DEITY AND MORALITY

DEITY AND MORALITY

With regard to the Naturalistic Fallacy

BURTON F. PORTER

London
GEORGE ALLEN AND UNWIN LTD
RUSKIN HOUSE   MUSEUM STREET

FIRST PUBLISHED IN 1968

This book is copyright under the Berne Convention. Apart from any fair dealing for the purposes of private study, research, criticism or review, as permitted under the Copyright Act, 1956, no portion may be reproduced by any process without written permission. Inquiries should be made to the publishers

© *George Allen & Unwin Ltd., 1968*

PRINTED IN GREAT BRITAIN
in 12 on 13 point Bembo type
BY UNWIN BROTHERS LTD
WOKING AND LONDON

ACKNOWLEDGEMENTS

I wish to tender my gratitude to the following individuals who served as catalysts for numerous ideas expressed in this work.

Professor Gilbert Ryle, Waynflete Professor of Metaphysical Philosophy in the University of Oxford, Professor R. M. Hare, White's Professor of Moral Philosophy and Fellow of Corpus Christi College, Oxford, the Rt Rev. Ian Ramsey, Bishop of Durham, Mr Basil Mitchell, Tutor in Philosophy, Keble College, Oxford, Professor A. D. Woozley, Professor of Moral Philosophy in the University of St Andrews, and Rev. Professor N. H. G. Robinson, Professor of Systematic Theology in the University of St Andrews.

CONTENTS

ACKNOWLEDGEMENTS   *page*

I. THE NATURALISTIC FALLACY   11
  A. *The Nature of the Fallacy*   11
  B. *The Application of the Fallacy*   14

II. DAVID HUME   25
  A. *Hume's Philosophical Position*   25
  B. *Hume's Theological Position*   32

III. DIVINE COMMAND, GOODNESS AND OBEDIENCE   42
  A. *Hume's Fallacy and Theological Naturalism*   42
  B. *Kierkegaard's 'Paradox of Faith'*   48

IV. DEITY AND MORALITY   58
  A. *Mediaeval Attitudes*   58
  B. *Contemporary Thoughts*   64

V. THE DOCTRINE OF INEFFABILITY   73
  A. *Mystical Knowledge*   73
  B. *Rudolph Otto's 'Numinous'*   84

VI. RELIGIOUS DISCOURSE AND POETIC LANGUAGE   90
  A. *Revelation and Inspiration*   90
  B. *Myth and Images*   100

VII. THE 'LOGICAL PARALLELS' APPROACH TO RELIGIOUS LANGUAGE   110
  A. *Anomalistic Language and Analogy*   110
  B. *Religious Language: Its Logical Behaviour and Ontological Status*   111

VIII. 'GOD IS GOOD': AN ANALYTIC PROPOSITION   121
  A. *The Essential Goodness of God*   121
  B. *Connotation and Denotation*   126

IX. THE CONNOTATION OF PROPER NAMES   134
  A. *Proper Names and Descriptive Terms*   134
  B. *Proper Names and General Meaning*   139

Deity and Morality

	page
X. THE CONCEPT OF GOD	151
A. *Comparative Conceptions of Deity*	152
B. *Analytic Propositions: Real or Verbal*	156
APPENDIX: AN ANALYSIS OF THE KEY TERMS INVOLVED	159
A. *'Is', 'Fact' and 'Description'*	159
B. *'Ought', 'Value' and 'Normative'*	164
INDEX	172

Chapter I

THE NATURALISTIC FALLACY

―――――

A: THE NATURE OF THE FALLACY

The criticism which has since been labelled the naturalistic fallacy was first described by the eighteenth-century empircist David Hume, in a small but celebrated paragraph in his *Treatise of Human Nature*. This passage reads as follows:

'In every system of morality which I have hitherto met with, I have always remarked, that the author proceeds for some time in the ordinary way of reasoning, and establishes the being of a god, or makes observations concerning human affairs; when of a sudden I am surpriz'd to find, that instead of the usual copulations of propositions, *is* and *is not*, I meet with no proposition that is not connected with an *ought*, or an *ought not*. This change is imperceptible; but it is, however, of the last consequence. For as this ought or ought not, expresses some new relation or affirmation, 'tis necessary that it should be observed and explained; and at the same time that a reason should be given, for what seems altogether inconceivable, how this new relation can be a deduction from others, which are entirely different from it. But as authors do not commonly use this precaution, I shall presume to recommend it to the reader; and am persuaded that this small attention would subvert all the vulgar systems of morality, and let us see, that the distinction of vice and virtue is not founded merely on the relations of objects, nor is perceived by reason.'[1]

The standard interpretation of Hume's point is that non-moral premises cannot logically entail a moral conclusion. It is a common procedure in many moral systems to begin with statements of fact concerning God's commands, human behaviour, or the natural world. Then it is maintained that *because* of these facts men ought to act in a particular way; because something is the case certain consequences follow for human conduct. Nowell-Smith, in outlining this fallacy, says that the answers to practical questions are deduced or derived from statements about what men are and in fact do.² This is judged to be illegitimate reasoning since the conclusion of the syllogism contains something which is not in the premises, namely, a moral prescription. The introduction of an *ought* in the conclusion is invalid unless *oughts* (rather than facts) appear in the premises.

Now A. C. MacIntyre holds that Hume pronounced this fallacy with tongue-in-cheek; that he never intended it to be considered seriously. In support of this view he states '... if the current interpretation of Hume's views on *is* and *ought* is correct, then the first breach of Hume's law was committed by Hume; that is, the development of Hume's own moral theory does not square with what he is taken to assert about *is* and *ought*'. He argues further that 'it would be very odd if Hume did affirm the logical irrelevance of facts to moral judgments for the whole difference in atmosphere—and it is very marked—between his discussions of morality and those of, for example, Hare and Nowell-Smith springs from his interest in the facts of morality. His work is full of anthropological and sociological remarks ...'³

I am inclined to the view that Hume was sincere in his belief that the passage from *is* to *ought* is logically barricaded, but that this did not prevent him from occasionally committing the blunder which he himself described. However, that is neither here nor there. For our present purposes, I think we can adopt the following position: whether or not Hume was sincere in claiming to unearth a basic fallacy, and whether or not, assuming it to be valid, he stands charged with it, the very fact that numerous others have seized upon it as the disclosure of an authentic fallacy is sufficient justification for regarding it seriously. Thus we can take Hume's statement as a prototype of the view which countless others maintain even if Hume did not.

However, let us now return to the main stream of our inquiry.

The Naturalistic Fallacy

Unfortunately for our task, Hume was not the only philosopher who is historically attributed with presenting this fallacy. A finding similar to that of Hume and actually coined *the naturalistic fallacy*, was repeatedly mentioned by G. E. Moore in *Principia Ethica*, in his polemical passages against naturalistic and metaphysical systems of ethics. Witness the following extracts:

'The naturalistic fallacy consists in the contention that good means nothing but some simple or complex notion that can be defined in terms of natural qualities.'[4]

In another section of the book he states the fallacy in greater detail:

'A mistake of this simple kind has commonly been made about *good*. It may be true that all things which are good are *also* something else, just as it is true that all things which are yellow produce a certain kind of vibration in the light. And it is a fact, that Ethics aims at discovering what are those other properties belonging to all things which are good. But far too many philosophers have thought that when they named those other properties, they were actually defining good; that these properties in fact were simply not *other* but absolutely and entirely the same with goodness. This view I propose to call the *naturalistic fallacy*.'[5]

There can be little doubt that a certain similarity exists between these 'fallacies', both of which bear the label the *naturalistic fallacy*, however, some writers have supposed that they are identical. That is to say, it has been maintained that Moore's naturalistic fallacy is the same as that to which Hume pointed of attempting to derive or deduce an *ought* from an *is*. (Iris Murdoch seems to make this mistake in *The Nature of Metaphysics*.) This is a confusion, although of a forgivable sort since it is encouraged by Moore's misnomer of the fallacy which he elucidated. Moore, in fact, admits this point, that his title is inappropriate, but replies 'I do not care about the name: what I do care about is

13

the fallacy'. This reply, however, is not sufficient justification for what is in effect a highly misleading label.

Moore's version actually has both a broader application and an O. Henry twist. The point it makes is not against naturalists *per se*, but against any theory which equates or syncretizes any two notions logically distinct. As A. R. White points out, 'If following Moore, we divide all notions into natural and non-natural, there are mathematically four varieties of this failure to distinguish two notions, namely, by identifying (1) a natural with another natural notion, (2) a non-natural with another non-natural notion, (3) a natural with a non-natural notion, (4) a non-natural with a natural notion. Since Moore did consider *good* to be a non-natural notion, case (1) could not arise for *good*; and since case (2) is the identification of two non-natural notions, it would be misleading to give a fallacy committed here the name *naturalistic*.' In this way, he would have to limit the *name* 'naturalistic fallacy about good' to (3) and (4). This is the fallacy which Hume thought of as the confusion of *is* and *ought* or vice versa. . . . But to narrow the fallacy to (3) and (4) gives a misleading picture of Moore's method.'[6] Moore bears out this point when he states: 'It should be observed that the fallacy by reference to which I define Metaphysical Ethics is the same in kind; and I give it but one name, the naturalistic fallacy.'[7] And at another point, 'Even if (goodness) were a natural object, that would not alter the nature of the fallacy nor diminish its importance one whit.'[8]

In this work we shall concentrate upon Hume's version of the fallacy, i.e. the alleged impossibility of deriving value judgments from natural facts.

B: THE APPLICATION OF THE FALLACY

If the naturalistic fallacy is in fact a genuine fallacy in moral theory, then an extremely powerful and damaging idea must be confronted. For if moral philosophers are logically precluded from deriving moral values from naturalistic sources, that is deriving an *ought* from an *is*, values from facts, or evaluative conclusions from descriptive premises, then ethical theories cannot rest upon the descriptive facts of experience; they must be in some sense autonomous.

Moral judgments and prescriptions are certainly on a firmer footing when some aspect of public experience can be brought forward to serve as justification. If a moralist can say that X is desirable because it is desired, he is in a stronger position than the individual who declares that mankind possesses an intuitive assurance that X is a moral end. The naturalistic hedonist, for example, can point to such things as the catholicity of pleasure-seeking behaviours among men and the lower animals, the identification of the pleasurable and the good in numerous contexts, the customary presupposition of the legislator that pleasure should be fostered, etc. When challenged to support his contention that pleasure ought to be valued, the naturalistic hedonist can point to any or all of these facts.

The non-naturalist seems in a feeble position by comparison because he is confined to appeals to an arid rationalism or a vaguely-defined intuitive apprehension of goodness. Not only is the descriptive warrant more persuasive to what James calls the 'ingrained naturalism and materialism of mind', but it places ethics on a scientific footing. It may not be possible to achieve the certainty of the geometrician that Descartes desired, or the exactitude and precision of the physical sciences that Bentham sought, but at least the premises of moral syllogisms could be established by scientific means. All moral principles could discover their natural roots in data about the universe.

However, if the naturalistic fallacy is a legitimate and universally applicable criticism then all of these stable foundations are shattered. The naturalists are logically prevented from drawing upon the principal source of their strength.

Let us look briefly at the varieties of naturalistic ethical theories which are directly affected by this issue.

(a) In the first place the naturalistic hedonist is severely affected by this logical difficulty, for he declares that because it is an undeniable fact of experience that men do pursue pleasure and seek to avoid pain, we are justified in concluding that human beings should pursue pleasure and avoid physical or psychological pain.

To numerous hedonists as well as non-hedonists it appeared obvious that the chief concern of mankind is the securing of pleasure, satisfaction, or happiness. Since men seek only that which they value, and value only that which they seek, it could be inferred that men do in fact regard the pleasurable as the good. The hedonist could say further that they are fully warranted in this assumption; what is directly and generally regarded as good *is* good. Unless we embrace a doctrine of the inherent depravity of man, the position that our normal tendencies can be assumed to rightly direct our steps appears very persuasive.

To the Cyrenaics the momentary, intense pleasures which men pursued were to be preferred. The inward flow of particular sensual pleasures should remain unimpeded by paltry considerations such as dishonour or discomfort, because the good life was composed of just these intense moments.

> 'Come, fill the cup, and in the fire of Spring
> Your Winter-garment of Repentance fling:
> The Bird of Time has but a little way
> To flutter—and the Bird is on the Wing.'[9]

To the Epicureans the pursuit of pleasure is both natural and inevitable—two facts which provide a base for the doctrine that the attainment of maximum pleasure is the moral end of life. Although eschewing the Cyrenaic insistence upon the desirability of intense sensual pleasures, and positing *ataraxia* or tranquil happiness as the supreme good, nevertheless the central hedonistic values are retained. A correct moral inference seemed possible and preeminently sensible from the fact that all living creatures have a natural impulse to take delight in pleasure to the proposition that pleasure ought to be pursued. 'We call pleasure the beginning and end of the blessed life. For we recognize pleasure as the first good innate in us.'[10] Or again: 'every pleasure because of its natural kinship to us is good even as every pain also is an evil'.[11]

The Naturalistic Fallacy

The Utilitarians in turn although eliminating the objectionably egoistic features of Greek hedonism by universalizing their ethical principles, nevertheless based their ethical hedonism on psychological hedonism. Jeremy Bentham clearly states this relationship in his *Introduction to the Principles of Morals and Legislation*:

'Nature has placed mankind under the guidance of two sovereign masters, pain and pleasure. It is for them alone to point out what we ought to do, as well as to determine what we shall do. On the one hand the standard of right and wrong, on the other the chain of causes and effects are fastened to their throne.'[12]

John Stuart Mill's bald statement of this connection is as follows:

'... the sole evidence it is possible to produce that anything is desirable, is that people do desire it.... No reason can be given why the general happiness is desirable except that each person, so far as he believes it to be attainable, desires his own happiness. This, however, being a fact, we have not only all the proof which the case admits of, but all which it is possible to require, that happiness is a good....'[13]

Both Bentham and Mill therefore can be seen to embrace the principle that human behaviour is always motivated by pleasure and they employ this as the logical basis for their Utilitarian prescriptions. Like Callicles in Plato's *Gorgias*, the pleasurable and the good are thought to be identical.

(b) In a similar manner the Stoics, who were the arch intellectual rivals of the Epicureans, claimed to have discovered their values full-blown in certain natural facts. Zeno, Seneca, Epictetus and the Emperor Marcus Aurelius Antoninus all claimed that man could achieve the good by discovering what nature sought and ordering his life in accordance with it. The natural was thought equivalent to the good. ' "Life in agreement with nature" (or living agreeably to nature) was the end of life.' ...

'living virtuously is equivalent to living in accordance with experience of the actual course of nature'.[14]

And nature was not regarded as a vast purposeless limbo but rather a harmonious order, shot throughout with rational principles and moving intelligently towards a destiny. Therefore conformity to nature meant agreement and active cooperation with all that life presented. The virtuous man recognized this fact and rationally controlled his conduct, subordinated his passions and aspirations in order to live in tune with nature. He did not flail against the apparent vicissitudes of life because he recognized a larger providence transforming ordinary existence. Like Plato and Aristotle, the Stoics exhalted the rational life which would master unruly desires and lead to self-possession and tranquillity.

However, when the Stoic's argument is logically dissected, here again the implicit and central moral derivation violates the naturalistic fallacy. Stripped of all rhetorical embellishments the argument appears as follows:

Nature wills X
Therefore X is good

or

X conforms to Nature
Therefore X is desirable

(c) A kindred nature theory, Evolutionary ethics, displays the same type of reasoning. Here, in fact, the most blatant derivation of an ethical system from descriptive information about nature occurs.

Herbert Spencer is most closely associated with this theory, however, Charles Darwin implicitly and explicitly provided the background for Spencer's speculations in his writings. Darwin wrote, 'The term, general good, may be defined as the rearing of the greatest number of individuals in full vigour and health, with all their faculties perfect, under the conditions to which they are subjected ... it would be advisable ... to take as the standard of morality, the general good or welfare of the community....'[15]

Furthermore, in the chapter on the Mental Powers and on the Moral Sense, Darwin declares that this evolutionary end, of rearing and preserving healthy vigorous individuals, could be brought about by mutual justice and consideration among men. Since human beings possessed a capacity for sympathy and were able to retain past experiences, social justice was thereby enabled to flourish.

To Herbert Spencer the concept of evolution adequately explained the nature of the universe and provided the foundation for morality. Change in the universe was always from a state of homogeneity to a state of heterogeneity; Evolution *meant* continual transformation toward greater and greater differentiation. The highest evolutionary state was the one of greatest heterogeneity and complexity. On the basis of this evolutionary concept Spencer declared that 'the conduct to which we apply the name good is the relatively more evolved conduct; and that bad is the name we apply to conduct which is relatively less evolved'.[16] In short, human conduct had to imitate the cosmic process; the dynamic movement of nature displayed to mankind a model for ethical conduct. Just as the Stoics maintained that human behaviour should conform to the rational will of the cosmos, so Spencer declared that men should pattern their lives upon the inexorable evolutionary process.

Strangely enough, Nietzsche inferred a very different ethical theory from the same facts of evolution. Instead of extracting the notions of progressively greater differentiation among organisms or mutual assistance, herd instinct and parental care present in the evolutionary stream, Nietzsche concentrated upon the self-assertive behaviour of animals in their struggle for existence. On the basis of this evidence Nietzsche prescribed a 'transvaluation of all values'. The Hebraic–Christian morality of cooperation, humility and love had to be abandoned and nature's values of ruthless aggression, combat and domination substituted in their place. These values were in accord with the evolutionary law of survival of the fittest and natural selection. By cultivating this *master-morality* rather than *slave-morality* humanity could re-enter the evolutionary flux.

(I might mention in passing that if the same evolutionary evidence can be used to justify a variety of ethical theories, it can be assumed that the inference is specious. As one philosopher put it, we cannot construct a moral theory on the strength of which way the frog will leap.)

All of these men, Darwin, Spencer, and Nietzsche as well as such figures as Peter Kropotkin, Olaf Stapledon, J. B. S. Haldane, and Julian Huxley, have adopted the evolutionary process as the touchstone for morality. An act is judged good only in so far as it conforms to certain facts of cosmic or organic evolution. And in this essential linkage between ethics and evolution a scientific account of moral behaviour is provided.

(*d*) I might mention briefly in this category the social approval theory which also interprets goodness in strictly naturalistic terms. According to its two major exponents, Emile Durkheim and Lucien Levy-Bruhl, a factual science of morals can be established by studying the formal and informal rules which actually prevail in society. The disapprobation of the community is indicative of the standards of morality entertained by its members. Society disapproves of actions which are not consonant with its sentiments (codified in specific rules) and consequently amasses a body of 'moral facts' which the moral scientist can examine. Levy-Bruhl and Durkheim are in thorough agreement on this point: '. . . all moral facts consist in a rule of sanctioned conduct'.[17] Ethical reality consists of 'ethical rules, obligations, laws, and whatever generally is contained in the conscience'.[18]

Moral science does not then prescribe changes in the moral rules in accordance with some transcendental *a priori* ('a pre-established general formula'), but it can correct deviations in a given society by a comparative study of cultural morality. '. . . only by comparing the results of these special studies shall we be able to extract the common characteristics of all moral rules, the constitutive properties of the law of ethics'.[19] Abnormalities will give way before evidence of the rules prevalent in 'normal' societies.

The function of the moral scientist then is to engage in a cross-cultural study of moral facts in order to discover the values which ought to be incorporated within a social structure (i.e. those displaying greatest frequency of occurrence), and those which need to be eliminated.

In this theory again we can discern a violation of the fact/value bifurcation. Goodness and rightness are unblushingly analysed into the prevailing, socially approved rules of behaviour.

(e) Most importantly for the purposes of this book, there is an ethical theory which C. D. Broad has called 'theological naturalism'.[20] Most theologians would endorse this theory in one form or another for it defines right strictly in terms of an omniscient omni-good deity's commands. Broad cites Paley as an historical representative of this view, I should imagine because of Paley's statements in the *Principles of Moral and Political Philosophy*, pp. 65 ff., however, the examples are endless.

The outstanding theologian Emil Brunner has quite typically stressed man's inability to construct an ethical system without recourse to deity. Man is inherently depraved and consequently produces a distorted, confused and fragmented moral code when he attempts an independent analysis of ethical behaviour. All man-centred, sin-tainted, ethical systems are destined to fail precisely because of their *terminus a quo*. Morality must originate with the all-pervading will and purpose of God. 'What God does and wills is good; all that opposes the will of God is bad.'[21] 'The Good is simply what *God* wills that we should do. . . .'[22] Sound ethical principles can only be achieved by discovering the genuine revelation of deity's purposes—the divinely sanctioned rules of human conduct.

Karl Barth likewise has given vigorous expression to a theological naturalism or a theological approbation theory. Like Brunner, Barth disparages the notion that man unaided is able to discover moral truth. Neither secular conscience nor religious consciousness can be trusted to discern moral direction. What's more, the vagaries of man's desires, his short-sightedness, selfishness and instinct of self-preservation, militate against a tenacious pursuit of moral purposes. Ethical knowledge and achievement are only possible through individual revelations of deity's sovereign will.

The revelation of God's will cannot be abstracted and fixed in a body of principles or universalized for mankind. However, morality wholly depends upon these revelations, most particularly the revelation in the person of Jesus. 'Through Him we are summoned to obedience and set in motion, and that does not mean the beginning of a *new* self-righteousness but the end of *all* self-righteousness. It does not mean that we are invited to have a new confidence in ourselves, but to put our entire confidence in Jesus Christ alone. It is solely in this confidence in Him that we shall be able to render the obedience required of us. By trusting in ourselves we could only become disobedient.'[23]

In this connection we might also mention Calvinism. Perhaps no other theological system so vehemently and persistently emphasizes the disabling force of original sin in man's life or the utter dependence of man on God for his salvation. John Calvin repeatedly states that man's fallen spirit can only be raised again to goodness by an omnipotent act of divine will. Nothing short of 'efficacious grace', regenerating man's spirit, will bring about right action. Man has the power (initially) to resist the influx of grace pressing upon his natural will, but he cannot win a state of grace by good works—he cannot perform right actions apart from God. Moral acts are in fact the *result* of divine grace cleansing and renewing man's soul.

Neither can man in his finitude and sinful condition comprehend the mind of God, the perfectly moral commandments of deity, the principle at work in the forewilled election or damnation of men. However, we can rest assured in the faith that deity's sovereign will is wholly moral no matter how arbitrary it appears. 'For the Will of God is the highest rule of righteousness, so that whatsoever He willeth, even for (undeserving predestination to eternal death) that He willeth it, ought to be taken for righteousness.'[24] (Parentheses mine.)

Further examples are readily accessible but superfluous. The

The Naturalistic Fallacy

theologians cited, although dissimilar in numerous respects, are united in their belief that morality is ultimately derived from the divine will. Behaving morally means recognizing that God's will is the criterion of righteousness and, more importantly, conforming to His laws.

This theory can be seen to be naturalistic (and, strangely enough, metaphysical as well), precisely because the commands which are in fact issued by deity are regarded as constituting the moral good for man. As a naturalistic ethical theory like hedonism, evolutionism, stoicism, social approbation and several others not discussed, it stands charged with David Hume's naturalistic fallacy. To reason that loving one's neighbour, for example, is right because it is approved by God, does violate the description/evaluation distinction.

Let's turn now to a consideration of the general background out of which Hume's troublesome criticism arose.

NOTES

Chapter I

1. Hume, D., *Treatise of Human Nature*, Edinburgh, Black, Tait and Tait, 1726, Vol. II, p. 236 (Book III, Part I, Section I).
2. Nowell-Smith, P. H., *Ethics*, Oxford, Basil Blackwell Ltd, 1957, p. 36.
3. MacIntyre, A. C., 'Hume on "Is" and "Ought" ', *The Philosophical Review*, Vol. LXVIII, October 1959, p. 455.
4. Moore, G. E., *Principia Ethica*, Cambridge, The University Press, 1959, p. 73.
5. Moore, G. E., *ibid.*, p. 10.
6. White, A. R., *G. E. Moore, A Critical Exposition*, Oxford, Basil Blackwell, 1958, p. 124.
7. Moore, G. E., *op. cit.*, p. 39. By 'Metaphysical Ethics' Moore means those ethical theories that 'use some *metaphysical* proposition as a ground for inferring some fundamental proposition of Ethics. They all imply, and many of them expressly hold, that ethical truths follow logically from metaphysical truth, that Ethics should be based on Metaphysics.' (p. 110) What C. D. Broad would call theological naturalism, G. E. Moore would call a metaphysical ethical theory.

8. Moore, G. E. *ibid.*, p. 14.
9. Omar Khayyám, *The Rubá'iyát*, trans. by Edward Fitzgerald, 1859 (Stanza 7).
10. Epicurus, 'Letter to Menoeceus', in *Epicurus, The Extant Remains*, trans. by Cyril Bailey, Oxford, Clarendon Press, 1926, p. 87.
11. *Ibid.*, p. 89.
12. Bentham, J., *Introduction to the Principles of Morals and Legislation*, London, W. Pickering, 1823, Vol. I, p. 1.
13. Mill, A. S., *Utilitarianism, Liberty and Representative Government*, London, J. M. Dent and Sons Ltd, 1910, pp. 32, 33 (Ch. IV).
14. Diogenes Laertius, *Lives and Opinions of Eminent Philosophers*, tr. by R. D. Hicks, Cambridge, Mass., Harvard University Press, 1925, Vol. II, p. 195.
15. Darwin, C., *The Descent of Man*, New York, D. Appleton and Co., 1897, p. 121.
16. Spencer, Herbert, *The Principles of Ethics*, New York, D. Appleton and Co., 1895, Vol. I, p. 15.
17. Durkheim, E., *On the Division of Labor in Society*, New York, The Macmillan Co., 1933, p. 425.
18. Levy-Bruhl, L., *Ethics and Moral Science*, tr. by E. Lee, London, Archibald Constable & Co., Ltd, 1905, p. 11.
19. Durkheim, E., *op. cit.*, p. 419.
20. Broad, C. D., *Five Types of Ethical Theory*, London, Routledge & Kegan Paul Ltd, 1930, p. 259.
21. Brunner, E., *The Divine Imperative, A Study in Christian Ethics*, tr. by Olive Wyon, Philadelphia, Pa., Westminster Press, 1947, p. 53.
22. *Ibid.*, p. 117.
23. Barth, K., *The Knowledge of God and the Service of God*, London, Hodder and Stoughton, 1938, p. 146.
  Conformity to the will of God as revealed to us in the life and teaching of Jesus is, of course, echoed by numerous other Christian theologians, e.g. the Schoolmen, Wesley, Niebuhr, Tillich, Bonhoeffer, etc.
24. Calvin, J., *The Institution of Christian Religion*, tr. by T. Norton, London, R. Wolfe and R. Harrison, 1561.
  A parallel statement by St Augustine is as follows: 'All things that exist, therefore, seeing that the Creator of them all is supremely good, are themselves good. . . . Nor can we doubt that God does well even in permission of what is evil. For he permits it only in the justice of His judgment. And surely all that is just is good.' St Augustine, *The Enchiridion*, tr. by J. F. Shaw, Edinburgh, 1892, Chs XII and XCVI respectively.

Chapter II
DAVID HUME

A: HUME'S PHILOSOPHICAL POSITION

The philosophy which Hume espoused has been variously labelled as scepticism, empiricism, phenomenalism, naturalism, and has even been called a type of theism. This heterogeneous group of titles testifies both to the scope and diversity of the subjects to which Hume addressed himself and the self-contradictory character of various facets of his views. They are also indicative of the dissimilar interests which Hume's philosophy can be shaped into serving.

That Hume was a sceptic can be ascertained by the representative case of his attitude toward causation. The credulous soul is hardly the one to doubt a necessary connection between cause and effect or to confine causal necessity to mental ideas erroneously transferred to objects when customarily viewing one to precede and be contiguous to the other. If that is not enough, we have Hume advising care in going beyond the most 'cautious observation of human life' and the plainest sense of experience; dismissing the external existence of perceived objects as delusive; declaring (with almost Freudian foreshadowing) that 'reason is and ought only to be the slave of the passions' and can never alone influence the will; and declaring the notion of a *self* as commonly understood to be a fiction, actually consisting of 'a bundle or collection of different perceptions, which succeed each other with an inconceivable rapidity and are in a perpetual flux and movement'. In Hume's almost cynical assertion that even *knowledge* eventually degenerated into *probability* we hear the echo of the alleged *Socratic doubt* (shared by Democritus, Anaxagoras, Empedocles and Cicero [Academic Questions]) that nothing can be ascertained, perceived or known with indefectible certainty. Of his four philosophic harangues published in 1742, *The Stoic, The Epicurean, The Platonist,* and *The Sceptic,* the last-named is the best and longest.

'But his scepticism was peculiar. It had well-defined limits. It extended only to the theory of knowledge, metaphysics and its pendent, natural theology, and not to ethics, politics or common life. What he doubted was the power of human reason to pronounce judgments on the highest themes. What he never doubted was the power of human instinct—or imagination as he often called it—to conduct and regulate our everyday affairs.'[1]

Yet neither imagination, which includes the instincts, natural dispositions and propensities of the mind, nor reason, which is of a mathematical or analytic stripe, can operate beyond the range of human experience. (In fact the attempt to bring matters of fact within the jurisdiction of reason inevitably ends in confusion and absurdity.) For this approach Hume can be justly labelled an empiricist.

That the label of phenomenalist is defensible can be determined by the fact that Hume held all our knowledge, belief and conjecture to begin and end with appearances. We cannot travel behind or beyond these appearances and to attempt to do so engenders muddle-headed and misleading thinking. Whether he attempted a *pure, sensory phenomenalism* as John Laird attempts to demonstrate,[2] or whether Hume's *pure phenomenalism* was *make-believe* as Whitehead maintains,[3] does not call into question the assumption that *a* basic phenomenalism is present in his philosophy.

However, when we examine the label naturalist, an insidious ambiguity in the referent of this term must be brought to the surface. Most people who would roundly pronounce, or denounce, Hume as a naturalist would not mean an ethical naturalist —that is, one of those moral philosophers whose theories of value are of an empirical nature, being centred in pleasure, approval, fitness, integration, evolutionary survival, etc., and is scientifically testable by virtue of this empirical core. They would not intend, in modern anachronistic jargon, that he specifically and explicitly held that judgments about rightness, wrongness, goodness and badness are utterances about the natural world, totally within the jurisdiction of science. They would mean that Hume is a firm believer in the essential terrestrial character of all things whatever, from mind to values; that he refused admission to a supernatural deity for justification or explanation of human affairs, holding fast to the dictum: *Nec Deus intersit nisis dignus vindice nodus Inciderit.* (And for Hume the difficulty was never worthy of such intervention.)

For Hume, contradictory directives issued by the imagination and the reason are perpetually in a state of war within human beings. The imagination dictated practical belief in such matters as the external world, independent of perceiving minds; the necessary connection between cause and effect; the motivating powers of reason and the mind, etc. Reason could not demonstrate any of these things. It could never reach a world independent of our perception, never locate a necessary, causal link in successive contiguous events and never capture that elusive, postulated entity called mind. However, this dilemma has natural roots. Reason itself is a *sine qua non* of being human, a determination of man. 'Nature, by an absolute and uncontrollable necessity, has determined us to judge as well as to breathe and feel; nor can we any more forbear viewing certain objects in a stronger and fuller light, upon account of their customary connection with a present impression, than we can hinder ourselves from thinking as long as we are awake, or seeing the surrounding bodies when we turn our eyes toward them in broad sunshine.'[4] And the imagination too has its natural watershed from which our animalistic instincts, dispositions and mental propensities pour forth.

Luckily for man, nature both produces this antinomy and indicates the escape hatch. In the final analysis we must inevitably rely upon the imagination for guidance in all practical affairs, otherwise despondency, impotence of action and intellectual schizophrenia will result. 'Most fortunately it happens, that since reason is incapable of dispelling these clouds, nature herself suffices to that purpose, and cures me of this philosophical melancholy and delirium, either by relaxing this bent of mind, or by some avocation, and lively impression of my senses, which obliterates all these chimeras. . . . Here then I find myself absolutely and necessarily determined to live, and talk, and act like other people in the common affairs of life . . . I may, nay I must, yield to the current of nature, in submitting to my senses and understanding. . . .'[5] 'The great subverter of Pyrrhonism or the excessive principles of scepticism is action and employment, and the occupations of common life.'[6]

Here, incidentally, lies the resolution of the apparent conflict in Hume's philosophy between naturalism and scepticism. Although 'a small tincture of Pyrrhonism' is useful in order not to think and act in an ultimately non-cogitative way, if man reflected or judged too searchingly and thereby became a thoroughgoing sceptic, the balance of his being was restored by the forces of his sensitive nature, exerting their practical, common-sensical demands; e.g. Hume intellectually rejected the notions of an efficacious reason, the self and causes, but in his ordinary sensitive beliefs became a *plebeian* as Cleanthes says, and positivistically assented to them. This bifurcation is certainly not an odd one. The Stoic sages in their exaltation might achieve a condition of universal doubt for short, intense periods, but only the arch-sceptic Pyrrho of Elis has to be protected from disregarding galloping horses in the street.

In the sense that Hume trusts the natural inclinations of his imagination and indeed regards nature as compelling him to do so, he is assuredly a naturalist in perhaps the same way as that of Henry David Thoreau, Jean Jacques Rousseau, James Fenimore Cooper and even Frank Norris, Emile Zola and Erskine Caldwell. And if Gellner is correct in regarding the reliance upon common usage of Oxford linguistic analysts to be a modern expression of the noble savage tradition, then Hume could also be classed among their number in that respect.[7] The subordination of reason to feeling and instinct may not be 'the determining factor in Hume's philosophy',[8] but it assuredly occupied an important position.

Hume's position on the subject of religion requires greater elucidation than the labels empiricist, phenomenalist, naturalist or sceptic which have been affixed to him. For the significance to theology, particularly to the moral ties between God and man, of the naturalistic fallacy which he depicted, has a definite place in this work. After a discussion of his religious views, we will be in a much better position to understand and relate this fallacy to his overall convictions.

To begin with, Hume's feelings towards contemporary Calvinism can be alliteratively described as disgust, doubt and deploration. Although he was raised within a cage of Calvinistic theology, he gratefully liberated himself from its oppressive constraints at an early age, even before he formulated the general outlines of his philosophy.[9] This conventionally respectable religion of the masses was found by Hume to be mere vulgar superstition which stultified society—'a species of daemonism'. He came to regard the stringent Calvinistic tenets of the election of a few to glory and the remainder to reprobation, as exerting a needlessly baleful influence upon the people, terrorizing them with the fear that they would surely be the recipients of God's 'cruel and implacable vengeance'. When its basic presuppositions underwent rigorous philosophic scrutiny the sword of Damocles under which the people quaked in abject dread was found to be a chimera—an imaginary and vicious invention thrown up by a bogus system.

Hume extended his refined Pyrrhonism, or mitigated scepticism, to Christianity at large, although here he proceeded against his emotional inclinations rather than with them. (Previously his personal distaste and humanistic abhorrence of the more brutish features of Calvinism precipitated his logical investigation of its articles of faith.) Nevertheless, it is seldom disputed that Hume squarely rejected the Christian doctrine. Those few dogged souls who have attempted to make Hume out a Christian have had to resort to such gambits as claiming that his writings are not expositions of his own religious faith,[10] or that he held a variant Christianity, substantially different from that professed by the average believer, or that we can glimpse Hume's true position in a few significant passages in the *Dialogues*.

The first is highly doubtful, as a cursory glance at Hume's

biography adequately reveals: no private practice of Christianity can be discerned anywhere. Furthermore, Hume was not affected or braggadocio in his writings, and even hesitated to publish works which drew out the implications of his thoughts to the detriment of Christianity. He certainly would not sacrifice sincerity to the achievement of a pleasurably shocking technique even for the sake of the literary fame he so greatly coveted.

As for the second, this assumption can only be justified by such allegedly paradigm utterances as, 'the particle of the dove' in human nature must eventually vanquish 'the elements of the wolf and the serpent' which, if we magnify in a Platonic manner to the unit of society, is analogous to the dictum, 'the meek shall inherit the earth'. Yet this sort of Christian confidence is far from the heart of the Church's doctrine. It is a peripheral pronouncement echoed in other religions; assent to the articulated hope hardly constitutes a necessary condition (let alone a sufficient condition) of being a follower of Christ. We would surely be straining the bonds of Christianity to place Hume within its confines on the basis of such *en passant* remarks.

As for justification solely by reference to the *Dialogues*, we have already spoken of the unreliability of this procedure. Both the procedure and the claim are rendered increasingly absurd by the discovery that Hume contradicted these significant passages elsewhere. Thus we can assume, as A. E. Taylor, J. Y. T. Greig and John Laird do, that Philo is either insincere or non-representative of Hume's opinions when he says such things as 'To be a philosophic Sceptic is, in a man of letters, the first and most essential step towards being a sound, believing Christian.'[22] The significance of such utterances seems to lie more in the fact that they buttress incorrect inductions of this sort, than that they express Hume's true feelings.

Hume in fact specifically attacked Christianity in his writings on Miracles.[12] As Orr points out, 'Since, however, in that age, belief in revelation was supposed to be supported chiefly by the evidence of miracles, it remained for Hume . . . to subvert effectually that reputed foundation of the Christian religion.'[13] This is borne out by Hume when he states, 'The Christian

Religion not only was at first attended with miracles, but even at this day cannot be believed by any reasonable person without one'.[14] Since by a miracle Hume means 'a violation of the laws of nature'—those laws which 'firm and unalterable experience' has shown to be regular and uniform, he would include in the class such specifically Christian occurrences as water being turned into wine, stones becoming bread, lepers and blind men being cured of their respective afflictions, no less than such Old Testament events as the Red Sea parting, the sun standing still in the valley of Ajalon, and the walls of Jericho collapsing at Joshua's trumpet blast. In arguing against the possibility of miracles he would also be attacking such fundamental Christian notions as the *logos* made flesh, the resurrection, the ascension, the second coming, and the immortality of the soul.

In substance, Hume's professedly 'decisive' argument against miracles is that a complete induction based on *all* previously experienced instances of the kind can never be overturned by testimony (itself a mode of experience) to what, as miraculous, is *ex hypothesi*, contrary to this induction—i.e. 'a weaker evidence [numerically considered) can never destroy a stronger'.[15] Although this argument has come in for much needed criticism, it cannot be doubted that Hume regarded it as 'entire', valid and decisive proof against this aspect of religious belief—'. . . an ever-lasting check to all kinds of superstitious delusion'. If it did not subsequently prove an 'everlasting check', eroding the foundations of belief in miracles, it certainly served to dissuade Hume from giving credence to such accounts and to the Christian edifice erected with miracles as its cornerstone. 'For Hume recognizes no uniqueness in Christianity such as would render it unseemly to place it, in discussion, on a level with the pagan religions of Greece and Rome.'[16]

It will be observed that Hume's opposition to Christianity takes a circumlocutory form. He does not attack orthodox Christianity directly, any more than he strikes down religion directly. Yet one should not be deceived into thinking, as some have done (e.g. Amelia H. Stirling), that he is only attacking religion's popular, superstitious and/or fanatical (zealous) forms. So much is encompassed within the Venn-like circles of these terms that, as Kemp-Smith remarks, 'it is far from clear what it is that remains when these are discounted'.[17]

B: HUME'S THEOLOGICAL POSITION

In regard to Hume's general theological position, James Orr rightly remarks: 'It is significant that nearly every modern theorist on the subject of religion—deist, pantheist, agnostic, pessimist, believer in a limited God, and believer in no God at all—can find his share in Hume, and fortify himself by his reasonings.'[18] However, this is not to say that Hume, acting inconsistently, buttressed contradictory positions at various stages of his public and private writings (although a philosophic development which cut across entrenched positions would be more desirable in the interest of academic honesty than an egotistical insistence upon consistency), but that various factions have extracted passages favourable to them from the multitudinous array of Hume's utterances, and erroneously (almost entirely) canonized Hume in their respective denominations.

That Hume is so elastic and malleable in religious matters is due in large part to his *Dialogues Concerning Natural Religion* in which the prime opponents, Philo and Cleanthes, are made vehicles for the expression of various types of views. Some of these views are of a classical form, some give utterance to the arguments of contemporary deism, and some embody Hume's peculiar brand of *Enlightenment* scepticism toward religion. These writings at once provide a virtual cornucopia of theological arguments to which diverse sects can lay claim, and seriously confuse the search for Hume's own position.

At first glance it would seem that Philo would be the mouthpiece for Hume's beliefs. His method of approaching questions is compatible with Hume's *modus operandi*; the type of scepticism at which he arrives smacks of Hume's own conclusions; and many of his utterances can find their counterparts in Hume's other writings. Kemp-Smith takes Philo's statement at the close of the final section of the *Dialogues* as being the sole passage in all of

Hume's writings in which he outspokenly declares 'the only knowledge of God that he is prepared to allow'.[19] What is more, he roundly contends that 'Philo, from start to finish, represents Hume'.[20]

Yet Cleanthes also appears to have a share of Hume's opinions and might be said to express the positive side of his nature. In a letter to Gilbert Elliott, Hume states, 'You would perceive by the sample I have given you that I made Cleanthes the hero of the dialogue: whatever you can think of to strengthen that side of the argument will be most acceptable to me'.[21] Moreover, the three protagonists are characterized in the introduction with the remarks 'the accurate philosophical turn of Cleanthes', 'the careless scepticism of Philo', and 'the rigid inflexible orthodoxy of Demea'.[22] Pamphilus's summation of the relative merits of the disputants' arguments reads, 'upon a serious view of the whole, I cannot but think, that Philo's principles are more probable than Demea's; but that those of Cleanthes approach still nearer to the truth'.[23]

In the light of this contradictory evidence it seems prudent to resort to Hume's other, more direct works before attributing to one or the other of the characters the dramatic presentation of Hume's ideas. When we do, we find that Philo and Cleanthes irregularly alternate in playing the role of Hume; they both represent phases of his mental development, some of which are transient and some of which are permanent. Thus to assume that either one alone carries the full burden of Hume's theological conclusions is to adopt a superficial and distorted view.[24]

This difficulty need not concern us in ferreting out Hume's thoughts on the ontological argument for the existence of God. When Demea puts forward 'that simple and sublime argument *a priori*' (propounded by Anselm, Bonaventure, Descartes, Leibnitz, Wolff and Hegel) of 'a necessarily existent Being, who carries the *reason* of his existence in himself; and who cannot be supposed not to exist without an express contradiction',[25] Philo and Cleanthes are united in expeditiously rejecting it. The criticism of this fallacious argument which is then offered has its roots in the *Enquiry*, where the fundamental distinction is made between 'Matters of Fact' and 'Relations of Ideas' (Sec. IV, Part I.)[26] In this section Hume claims that 'Nothing that is distinctly conceivable implies a contradiction'. Those things which are conceivable as existent entities are also conceivable as non-existent entities. There is not any being, therefore, the non-existence of which implies a contradiction. Anselm's formulation of God as *id quo maius cogitari nequit* thus has no meaning; neither does Descartes' argument that the very notion of God, the most perfect Being, carries existence with it as necessarily as the analytic concept of triangularity includes the equality of the sum of its angles to two right angles. For necessity is attributable to valid judgments only; it is not attributable to things.[27] 'Matters of fact (or Relations of Ideas) are not ascertained in the same manner; nor is our evidence of their truth, however great, of a like nature with the foregoing. The contrary of every matter of fact is still possible.'[28]

This point is echoed in slightly softer tones by Berkeley in his emphasis upon the arbitrariness of natural connections. It found its most profound expression, however, in Kant, and has not been put forward seriously in its Cartesian form since the publication of the *Critique of Pure Reason*. To the affirmation that the highest perfection in one's mind must necessarily include real existence, Kant retorted that the concept of the highest perfection lacks nothing as a concept when it lacks real existence in the outside world; existence is not an addition to the content of any idea. To attempt to add reality to a concept would be like trying to 'improve' the value of a hundred imaginary dollars by adding a real one from one's pocket. It is an impossible feat. 'Being is evidently not a real predicate, that is, a conception of something that is capable of being added to the conception of a thing . . . I add nothing to my conception, which expresses merely the possibility of the object, by simply placing its object before me in thought, and saying that it *is*.'[29]

Let me conclude this topic with Gilbert Ryle's recent remark that 'one of the biggest advances in logic that has been made since Aristotle (is) Hume's and Kant's discovery that particular matters of fact cannot be the implicates of general propositions, and so cannot be demonstrated from *a priori* premises'.[30] On this basis, a demonstrative knowledge of God and rational apologetics are undermined.

To Kant, the ontological argument for the existence of God was at the heart of the 'dogmatic' position of traditional theology; to Hume, the teleological argument or the argument from design was the 'chief or sole argument for a divine existence'. Yet Hume and Kant are one in disparaging the ontological proof (as did Aquinas and Gaunilo earlier) and admitting a great deal of esteem for the argument from design. Kant, although repudiating the teleological argument, nevertheless pays it the following high tribute: 'This proof always deserves to be mentioned with respect. It is the oldest, the clearest and the most accordant with the common reason of mankind . . . It suggests ends and purposes, where our observation would not have detected them by itself, and extends our knowledge of nature by means of the guiding-concept of a special unity, the principle of which is outside nature. This knowledge . . . so strengthens the belief in a supreme Author of nature that the belief acquires the force of an irresistible conviction.'[31]

In the *Dialogues Concerning Natural Religion*, Hume seems to my mind to be endorsing the argument from design in an important and formal sense. In saying this I am disagreeing with the authoritative commentator Kemp-Smith and accepting the view that in the concluding portion of the *Dialogues* Hume: 'seems to lay aside his sceptical mask and let us see for a few moments his individual belief on the great question in debate'; that his conclusions are 'neither due to the literary art of the dialogue nor is it an insincere concession to public opinion'.[32]

In the concluding section (Part XII) Philo abandons his former scepticism and declares his 'unfeigned sentiments'. 'A purpose, an intention, a design strikes everywhere the most careless, the most stupid thinker; and no man can be so hardened in absurd systems, as at all times to reject it.'[33] This statement comes somewhat as a surprise in regard to the previous debate in the *Dialogues*, but it is perfectly consistent with Hume's utterances in other works, e.g. the opening paragraph of his *Natural History of Religion.* Here the existence of God as established by the teleological proof goes unquestioned; it is presupposed in examining the origin of religion. 'The whole frame of nature bespeaks an Intelligent Author; and no rational inquirer can, after serious reflection, suspend his belief a moment with regard to the primary principles of genuine theism and Religion.'[34] Also in a note appended to the *Treatise* he says: 'The order of the universe proves an omnipotent mind. Nothing more is requisite to give a foundation to all the articles of religion.'[35] Hume's final revision of the *Dialogues* in 1776 contains the following remarks by Philo, marked for insertion: Philo declares that disputes over this subject do not concern meaning but are 'merely verbal'. The basic analogy is never at issue, merely the *degree* to which the 'original intelligence' is analogous to human reason.[36]

However, after granting the existence of the deity on teleological grounds, Hume goes on to sap his admission of all strength and practical utility. In the *Enquiry Concerning Human Understanding* Hume briefly assumes the circumspect dialogue form to forcibly argue that if the argument from design is valid, it only establishes the existence of a deity or deities possessing the 'precise degree of power, intelligence, and benevolence, which appears in their workmanship. . . . The supposition of further attributes is mere hypothesis; . . . The knowledge of the cause being derived solely from the effect, they must be exactly adjusted to each other; and the one can never refer to anything farther, or be the foundation of any new inference and conclusion.'[37] In other words, if God can be demonstrated as sufficiently powerful to create the world, we cannot on these grounds suppose that He also created the universe or is omnipotent; if we declare that God's earthly productions display a benevolent or wise nature, we cannot by 'exaggeration and flattery' prove further that He is all good and omniscient. Arguing in this specious way, a mischievous sophist could just as readily magnify God's defects in nature into an all-ignorant being, or by the same process infer Him to be totally malevolent. He cannot be proved to possess more or less power than He displays, more or less benevolence, more or less knowledge. And a deity constructed on this skeletal framework is hardly an acceptable object of worship, veneration and obedience; Hume's rational piety and 'genuine Theism' with the argument from design as its logical basis is seen to be a hollow vessel indeed.

Furthermore, in the *Dialogues*, Hume draws the line of human knowledge of God as deduced from the order and design in nature, a *physico-theological proof*, to use Kant's term. The works of nature irresistibly suggest a Being who bestowed existence and order on the universe according to a regular plan or connected system, but when one contemplates the conduct of events, or what we may call the plan of a particular providence, one cannot infer the will or moral attributes of God, a moral government or order of the universe, the moral responsibility of man towards his creator, or in fact anything which affects human life. There is a supreme being in the universe, but we cannot say what the nature of this being is except that it is like human intelligence. We have not any basis, in the light of this, for behaving other than we do under the inspiration of our common morality, and we should not imagine that what is pleasing to us, moves us, influences us, etc., holds true for God as well. '. . . the whole of Natural Theology resolves itself', in Philo's concluding words, 'into one simple, though somewhat ambiguous, or at least undefined proposition, that the causes of order in the universe probably bear some remote analogy to human intelligence; If this proposition be not capable of extension, variation, or more particular explication: If it affords no inference that affects human life, or can be the source of any action or forbearance: And if the analogy, imperfect as it is, can be carried no farther than to the human intelligence; and cannot be transferred, with any appearance of probability, to the other qualities of the mind: If this really be the case, what can the most inquisitive, contemplative, and religious man do more than give a plain, philosophical assent to the proposition, as often as it occurs; and believe that the arguments, on which it is established, exceed the objections which lie against it?'[38]

This conclusion is surely not what those who have contended for the existence of God have meant by that doctrine. Theism in its proper sense is a doctrine which affects our whole view of the universe and man's conduct in it. Hume's finite God, of bare, physical proportions upon whom we are neither morally nor physically dependent, is devoid of any significance and theological utility. The parable called to mind by Huxley, of the ass laden with salt who took to the water, is particularly apt to illustrate the nature of Hume's theism; it 'dissolves away in the dialectic river, until nothing is left but the verbal sack in which it was contained'. It becomes in fact a deism of the most trivial and impotent sort, as Warburton (to Hume's annoyance) claimed. Philo's admission of this sort of *theism* is hardly inconsistent with the previous tenor of his argument when we examine the barren nature of this attenuated theism to which he adheres.

NOTES

Chapter II

1. Greig, J. Y. T., *David Hume*, London, Jonathan Cape, 1937, p. 14.
2. Laird, J., *A Study in Moral Theory*, London, Allen & Unwin, Ltd, 1926, pp. 25-63.
3. Whitehead, A. N., *Process and Reality*, Cambridge, The University Press, 1929, p. 240.
4. Hume, D., *Treatise of Human Nature*, p. 183.
5. Hume, D., ibid., p. 269.
6. Hume, D., *An Enquiry Concerning the Human Understanding*, Edinburgh, Black, Tait and Tait, 1726 Oxford, The Clarendon Press, 1894, pp. 158-9.
7. Gellner, E., *Words and Things*, London, Victor Gollancz Ltd, 1959, p. 106.
8. Kemp-Smith, N., 'The Naturalism of Hume', *Mind*, N. S., Vol. XIV, No. 54, April 1905, p. 150.
9. See Orr, J., *David Hume and His Influence on Philosophy and Theology*, Edinburgh, J. & J. Clark, 1903, p. 2; Taylor, A. E., *The Faith of a Moralist*, Series I, London, Macmillan & Co., 1930, p. 164; Kemp-Smith, N., *Hume's Dialogues Concerning Natural Religion*, Oxford, The Clarendon Press, 1935, p. 1.
10. Caldecott, A., *The Philosophy of Religion*, London, Methuen & Co., 1901, p. 374.
11. Kemp-Smith, N., *op. cit.*, p. 282.
12. For a thorough criticism of Hume's views on miracles see Taylor, A. E., 'David Hume and the Miraculous' in *Philosophical Studies*, London, Macmillan & Co., 1934, p. 330.

13. Orr, J., *op. cit.*, p. 209.
14. Hume, D., *Enquiry Concerning Human Understanding*, p. 131.
15. Kemp-Smith, N., *op. cit.*, p. 59n. Mill distilled this down to mean that no testimony can ever prevail against a complete induction.
16. Kemp-Smith, N., *op. cit.*, p. 13.
17. *Ibid.*, p. 24.
18. Orr, J., *op. cit.*, p. 192.
    L. A. Selby-Bigge makes the following remarks about Hume's philosophic writings: 'His pages, especially those of the Treatise, are so full of matter, he say so many different things in so many different ways and different connexions, and with so much indifference to what he has said before that it is very hard to say positively that he taught or did not teach this or that particular doctrine. . . . This makes it easy to find all philosophies in Hume, or, by setting up one statement against another, none at all.' Hume, D., *Enquiry Concerning the Human Understanding*, p. vii.
19. Hume D., *Dialogues Concerning Natural Religion*, p. 26.
20. *Ibid.*, p. 76.
21. Burton, J. H., *Life and Correspondence of David Hume*, Edinburgh, Wm. Tait, 1866, Vol. I, pp. 331–2.
22. Hume, D., *op. cit.*, p. 159.
23. Hume, D., *ibid.*, p. 282.
24. This conclusion is not the one endorsed by the most respected commentators on Hume. Below is a short list of persons who have addressed themselves to this interpretation problem, and have come down positively in favour of Philo or Cleanthes as representing Hume. Those who argue for Pamphilus are in effect championing Cleanthes, since he, as adjudicator, awards the victory to the argument of Cleanthes.
    (1) Those who identify Hume with Philo:
      Laird, J., *Hume's Philosophy of Human Nature*, London, Methuen & Co., Ltd, 1932, p. 297.
      Greig, J. Y. T., *David Hume*, London, Jonathan Cape, 1934, p. 237.
      Orr, Jas., *David Hume*, Edinburgh, J. & J. Clark, 1903, p. 20.
      Stephen, Sir Leslie, *English Thought in the 18th Century*, London, Smith & Elder, 1776, 3rd ed., 1902, Ch. VI.
      Rose, Wm., *Monthly Review*, London, December 1779, Vol. lxi, p. 343. (The first reviewer of the *Dialogues*.)
      Huxley, T. H., *David Hume*, London, Macmillan & Co., 1887, Ch. VIII.
      Kemp-Smith, N., *Hume's Dialogues Concerning Natural Religion*, Oxford, 1935, Ch. V, Appendix D, pp. 122 ff.
      Paulsen, Friedrich, *Dialoge über natürliche Religion*, Leipzig, 3rd ed., 1905, pp. 19–20.
    (2) Those who identify Hume with Cleanthes:

Fraser, A. C., *Philosophy of Theism*, First Series, Edinburgh, W. Blackwood, 1895, pp. 209, 215-18, 240.
Windelband, W., *A History of Philosophy*, trans. by Jas. H. Tufts, New York, Macmillan & Co., 1896, pp. 494, 498.
Jodl, Friedrich, *Leben und Philosophie David Hume*, Gekronte Preisschrift, Halle, 1872, p. 175.
Stewart, Dugald, *The Collected Works of Dugald Stewart*, Edinburgh, J. & J. Clark, 1854, Vol. I, N. ccc, p. 179.
Laing, B. M., *David Hume*, London, Ernest Benn, 1932, p. 179.
Pringle-Pattison, A. S., *The Ideal of God*, Oxford, 1917, p. 15.
Burton, J. H., *Life and Correspondence of David Hume*, Edinburgh, Wm Tait, 1866, Vol. I, p. 329.
McEwen, B., *Hume's Dialogues Concerning Natural Religion*, Edinburgh, W. Blackwood, 1907, Intr., p. xxxix.
Hendel, C. W., *Studies in the Philosophy of David Hume*, Princeton, 1925, pp. 306-7.
Metz, Rudolf, *David Hume, Leben und Philosophie*, Stuttgart, 1929, pp. 345 ff.
Leroy, André, *La Critique et la Religion chez David Hume*, Paris, 1934, pp. 289-93, 369.
Taylor, A. E., 'Theism', *Hastings Encyclopedia of Religion and Ethics*, Edinburgh, J. & J. Clark, 1921, Vol. XII, p. 273.
25. Hume, D., *Dialogues Concerning Natural Religion*, p. 232.
26. Butler's distinction between 'abstract truth' and 'matter of fact' is quite similar to Hume's division. See Butler, J., *The Analogy of Religion*, London, J., J. & P. Knapp, 1736, (Part II, viii).
27. The second form in which Descartes casts the ontological proof is slightly more convincing. By saying that the idea of an infinite and perfect God cannot be made known to man by any finite object, he is suggesting the currently palatable notion that God is the sufficient reason of the idea of himself in man. Anselm also seems to be saying at times that among the notions in man's mind, the notion of Perfect Being has the power of assuring man about its existence.
28. Hume, D., *Enquiry Concerning the Human Understanding*, p. 25.
29. Kant, I., *Critique of Pure Reason*, trans. by John Watson, Glasgow, James Maclehose & Sons, 1901, pp. 208-9 (Bk. II, Ch. III, Sec. 4). Hegel and others have attempted to resuscitate the ontological proof by claiming that the idea of God as the absolute being is in a different position from a thing like a sum of money. God has to be thought as existing; 'His notion involves being'. I shall later attempt to demonstrate that His notion involves moral obligation.
30. Ryle, G., 'Mr Gollingwood and the Ontological Argument', *Mind*, N. S., Vol. XLIV, No. 174, April, 1935, p. 142.

31. Kant, I., *The Critique of Pure Reason*, trans. by N. Kemp-Smith, London, Macmillan & Co., Ltd., 1933, p. 520 (A624). (B652).
32. Pringle-Patterson, A. S., *op. cit.*, p. 14.
33. *Dialogues*, p. 264. Kemp-Smith takes the view that Hume is here underlining the powerful emotional impact of the argument—its 'overwhelming impression'—while still maintaining that feeling is 'an untrustworthy guide'. He cites the following passage in support of this stand, italicizing the latter portion: 'The most obvious conclusion surely is in favour of design; and it requires time, reflection and study, to summon up those frivolous, though abstruse, objections, which can support infidelity.' (p. 191).
    Yet even if we interpreted this sentence as Kemp-Smith does, and regarded it as of over-riding importance, we might still reach far different conclusions than that Hume took the whole to be 'a riddle, an enigma, an inexplicable mystery'. There seems in fact to be greater support for *at least* saying that Hume acknowledged a certain emotional propensity toward and an almost overpowering force in the teleological argument which could well serve as an hypothesis (of more or less probability) for God's existence, but was incapable of formal demonstration.
34. 'The Natural History of Religion' in *The Philosophic Works of David Hume*, London, Black & Tait, 1826, Vol. IV, p. 435.
35. Hume, D., *A Treatise of Human Nature*, ed. by L. A. Selby-Bigge, op cit., p. 172 (Book I, Part III, Sec. 14).
36. C. W. Hendel remarks at this point that 'There is no reason to doubt that this was the sincere expression of Hume's final opinion. The entire concluding Part of the *Dialogues* is in the tone of a confession of faith. And the work itself . . . was to be issued to the world only after the death of the author, who would then have nothing to gain or fear from man's suffrage or displeasure.' Hendel, C. W., *op. cit.*, p. 399.
37. Hume, D., *Enquiry Concerning Human Understanding*, p. 137 (Sec. XI, 106).
38. Hume, D., *Dialogues Concerning Natural Religion*, p. 281.

Chapter III

DIVINE COMMAND, GOODNESS AND OBEDIENCE

A: HUME'S FALLACY AND THEOLOGICAL NATURALISM

Hume's theological position thus implicitly denies God's providence. The concept of deity in the universe is an isolated and totally detached fragment of knowledge which does not exert any force upon the affairs of man. Although we must take God's power (as precisely displayed in His works) seriously into account when formulating metaphysical conceptions as to the origin and nature of the universe, His being does not, in fact, and by virtue of His finitude cannot, influence us in judgments on moral matters. We do not have to do what is expedient to secure His blessing or avoid His wrath, or perform epistemological acrobatics to determine His will. Indeed, He is negatively characterized as not being of such a nature to will or govern man's conduct. Unlike the traditional Christian view of God, Hume's deity does not issue moral exhortations, assign praise or blame, administer reproof, demand sacrifices or indicate moral pathways. If this deity is not a blind force, He is surely a seriously handicapped one.

Hume's conclusions on the relationship between deity and morality are strikingly duplicated in his treatment of the relationship between *is* and *ought*. That the theological implications of the absence of a necessary connection between the physically or spiritually existent and the morally advisable or obligatory are identical with the position just described need hardly surprise us. It is an interesting parallel to notice, however.

The theological implications of the *is/ought* bifurcation are as follows: 'No information about the nature of reality, or knowledge that there is a God and that He issues commands,[1] will by itself tell us what is good or what we ought to do. The statement, *God wills X*, is not a moral pronouncement. Before we know whether we ought to do *X*, we must know that what God wills is good. And in order to know what God wills is good, we should have to judge independently that it is good. That something is good is not entailed by God's willing it, for otherwise it would be redundant to ask, *Is what God wills good?* But this question is not redundant. *God wills X* or *God commands X* is not equivalent to *X is good*, as *X is a male parent* is equivalent to *X is a father*. *God wills it but is it good?* is not a senseless self-answering question like *Fred is a male parent, but is he a father?* The moral agent must independently decide that whatever God wills or commands is good.'[2]

The alert reader will ask at this point whether the writer of the above quotation is actually making a different point than the one which Hume draws our attention to in the now celebrated *is/ought* paragraph. The two points which such an objector would want to distinguish are (1) that human judgment, man's moral understanding of what is right, is an inescapable, prior condition of judging God benevolent and consequently worthy of obedience in moral matters, and (2) that we cannot logically or intelligibly determine any judgments of value from the nature of entities (such as God) which constitute the universe. Upon closer examination, however, these two seemingly different points are in fact one point, differently expressed.

Let us take the sentence cited above. Nielsen's objection to deriving *X is good* from *God wills X*, is that one must first judge whatever God wills to be good. In other words, *God wills X* therefore *X is good* is an enthymeme of the first order, which is logically defective until it is supplied with the major premise, *Everything that God wills is good*. The argument turns upon the assumption that (A), the major premise which requires to be inserted is a moral judgment, and (B) that according to rules of logical inference, the syllogism is a *non sequitur* without this premise. Supplying the unstated value judgment as the major-premise is a necessary condition for deducing a practical conclusion from the minor (*religious*) premise; the viability and validity of the argument hinges upon this insertion. And the fact that it is a *value judgment* which renders the argument explicable, which is the prime objective, is sufficient grounds for establishing the importance and priority of moral judgment to religious assent.

But is this not Hume's point as well? Are not the implications of Hume's position that it is illegitimate to reason from *God wills X* (which is here functioning primarily as a descriptive sentence) to *X is good*? Merely knowing that there is a God and that He issues moral injunctions is inadequate grounds for determining that these injunctions are *ipso facto* right. We have invalidly leaped from the descriptive to the evaluative. When we expand the abbreviated reasoning by supplying the major (moral) premise, we have changed the very nature of the syllogism—or rather laid bare its true nature. We can only avoid committing the *Naturalistic Fallacy* at the expense of exposing the argument as basically moral in character.

Therefore, if there is any difference between the point made by Nielsen (and others anxious to establish the priority of moral judgment to religious assent) and Hume, it is a trivial one of emphasis. Nielsen would have us notice that the minor premise, explicable by means of a value judgment as the major premise, is a religious one, and Hume would emphasize that it is a descriptive one. It is, of course, both; it is a descriptive *statement* of a religious claim. Hume would see in the fact that the argument is rendered moral in nature when the omitted premise is set in place, an important vindication of his contention that the passage from *is* to *ought* is logically barricaded; to Nielsen this apodeictic insertion points out the logical priority of moral discernment to obedience to God. Nielsen's position is in fact representative of the theological expression of the *is/ought* implications.

Let us now examine this theological point. The first recorded discussion of this issue occurs in the Euthyphro. Here the combatants, Socrates and Euthyphro, are said to meet immediately prior to the convocation of the Athenian court. There, Socrates is soon to defend himself in the face of various nebulous charges brought against him by Meletus (as reported in the *Apology*), while Euthyphro is prosecuting his father in the court for the crime of murder. Socrates inquires of the self-confident Euthyphro if he is so certain of the nature of piety as to entertain no doubts concerning the general propriety of his own conduct, i.e. for a son to bring his father to justice. After Euthyphro assures him that he is so convinced, Socrates begins to question him in what is (ironically) an attempt to learn this extraordinary knowledge. Socrates professes to be motivated by ignorance and immediate self-interest in doing so, for once having learned the nature of piety, he will be adequately armed against the charges of impiety facing him.

In the subsequent discussion Euthyphro flounders about attempting to define what piety is (definition being then regarded as a quasi-magical doorway to essence) and Socrates iconoclastically shows what piety is not. By means of the usual pointed questions, more and more definite answers are educed from Euthyphro, until the following crucial dilemma is posed: 'The point which I should first wish to understand is whether the pious or holy is beloved by the gods because it is holy, or holy because it is beloved of the gods.'[3]

This is a key question for the discussion of the nature of piety and an especially decisive one for the issues with which we are concerned. For as Heidel puts it: 'If holiness were holiness because the gods loved it, then the fact of the gods' loving an act would be the first essential point to determine in deciding whether the act was or was not holy; but if the gods loved holiness because it was holy, then its being holy would be a fact without the gods' loving it, and hence their loving it would not effect its nature'...[4] 'the one becomes lovable from the fact that it is loved, whereas the other is loved because it is in itself lovable'.

Euthyphro declares, or rather acquiesces to his adversary's forced conclusion, that piety 'is loved because it is holy, not holy because it is loved'.[6]

Although the argument concerning piety can and does proceed beyond this point, at this juncture Euthyphro is excluded from ultimately characterizing the nature of piety in terms of that which God loves. In defining piety in this way, Euthyphro has

Deity and Morality

merely drawn attention to an accidental attribute of piety rather than to its essential character; the fact that the gods love piety does not increase our knowledge of the nature of the concept (9E-11B).

This time-worn issue dealt with by Plato, and later Kant, Hume, and a number of modern writers including K. Nielsen, R. M. Hare, G. E. M. Anscombe, W. D. Falk, Wm R. Dennes, R. N. Smart, etc., is simply the permanent problem confronting the establishment of norms of value on a theory of deity—of claiming the nature of goodness to be ultimately determined by God. If we judge that religious evidence, written or revealed, has sufficiently established the truth or probability of the theory that an omniscient, omnipotent, omnipresent deity governs the universe, we are still not in a position to judge that whatever this God commands is therefore right. William R. Dennes expresses this point well when he states that 'the idea of good is prior to, and is not derivative from, the idea of deity' . . . 'If it were true, and known to be true, that an all powerful intelligence controls the universe; if besides we knew His commands and knew also that disobedience to them (even including His command to slay one's son on an altar) would lead to our destruction, it might indeed follow that obedience was expedient, but it would certainly not follow that obedience was right. In order that that should follow we require the further premise that deity is benevolent; that is, that deity wills not just whatever deity wills, but wills what is right.'[7] Human judgment is thus regarded as an inescapable and prior condition of asserting God as benevolent.

In a recent book, A. Victor Murray uses the myths of Prometheus and Faust to illustrate attempts at self-realization or self-assertion over an established order towards which a certain adolescent sense of helplessness is felt. The Prometheus myth as dealt with by Aeschylus is an object lesson in the sin of *hubris*—vain attempts to usurp the power or invade the sacred domain of deity. Goethe's *Faust* is a similar example of the sinful attempt to extend the frontiers of human knowledge beyond their appointed limits. The proud Xerxes in *The Persians*, the boastful Nebuchadnezzar (Daniel vii. 29), the arrogant King of

Assyria (Isaiah x) and, of course, the restless Oedipus relentlessly pursuing truth, are additional examples of individuals so intent upon controlling their destiny that they failed to perceive that the sword of Damocles has been set quivering. Murray makes the point that the didactic theme running throughout is that man must 'see the abyss and yet believe in God's mercy and grace' and 'that self-surrender is in fact *itself* self-realization.'[8]

Although these are major themes present in the above mentioned stories, there are also profound strains of a slightly different nature. All of these individuals experience the human dilemma of believing that the universe exhaustively provides for their wellbeing and yet withholds a portion of the salutary; they doubt the former although it seems indubitable and believe the latter although it appears incredible. Man desperately desires to convince himself with Leibniz that the pre-established harmony of the universe, chosen by God in perfect knowledge and goodness, is the best of all possible worlds; however, reflections upon this established order lead him to judge differently. Prometheus stole fire from the heavens when this gift was arbitrarily denied to man. Surely we must judge that Prometheus acted rightly, out of moral, humanitarian motives when he assumed the initiative and brought fire down to man. And what can we think of Zeus who denied a life-sustaining or comforting power to man, sent Pandora to earth with her box of evil to counterbalance this wrested blessing, and then tortured mankind's benefactor unmercifully. Is Prometheus blameworthy for presuming to judge and revolt against the supreme deity, or praiseworthy in relying upon his moral assessment of the situation? Surely we must affirm the latter. And was Prometheus justified in teaching man the art of architecture, writing, mathematics, navigation, medicine and astronomy, yet not justified in countermanding the orders of Zeus concerning the equally obvious boon of fire? Surely we must affirm that his questioning of Zeus's commands was justified, his judgment as to its wrongness was correct, and that he was morally right (if not prudential) in acting upon it.

However, here we are treading upon dangerous ground. For we are opening up the door to the possibility that there are occasions in which it is right to disobey deity; that *hubris* is not categorically evil but on occasions a positively desirable attitude. This rests upon the further assumption that deity does not will only that which is good but sometimes commands that which is not good. We are hereby establishing a precedent by reference to which Satan might be declared right in revolting against God in *Paradise Lost*, Eve justified in partaking of the forbidden fruit (assuming she was motivated by a quest for knowledge rather than acting in consequence of a morally weak character), and Faust right in reaching beyond the province of knowledge assigned to man. At the very least we cannot unconditionally condemn their actions by saying that they violated the will of God or opposed His judgment.

What is more, we cannot continue to praise traditionally praiseworthy figures such as St Paul, Abraham and Job strictly on the grounds of their absolute, unquestioning obedience to God. Having lost this criterion we might well conclude that Abraham was wrong in intending to sacrifice his son on God's instruction. Once obedience to God is no longer the absolute standard for conduct, an individual may be praiseworthy for *not obeying* God's command as well as praiseworthy in *disobeying* God's command.

B: KIERKEGAARD'S 'PARADOX OF FAITH'

Sören Kierkegaard, in an illustration which typifies his poetic technique and indirect method of communication, uses the story of Abraham to exemplify the meaning of absolute faith in deity. Kierkegaard sees in Abraham the classic case of a man whose belief in God is exposed to supreme stress and tension when he received an authoritarian imperative in direct contradiction to his reason, conscience and instincts of parental love. Abraham's individual faith was exemplary because he suspended his moral judgements or rather denied the ascendancy of his ethical sense altogether, in order to act in strict accordance with a creature's absolute duty to his Maker. In various parts of the Gospels it is implied that the essential failing of the Jews was moral pride;

Divine Command, Goodness and Obedience

they were more concerned with personal importance than with obeying God's will (e.g. St John v. 44). However, Abraham had the spiritual courage to resolve the *Paradox of Faith*—to believe that the *Individual* is superior to the *Universal*, the faith to believe that his relationship with the *Universal* was determined by his relationship with the *Absolute* (to use Hegelian–Kierkegaardian terms) rather than *vice versa*. As Abraham remained unfaltering in his intention to obey the will of God and sacrifice Isaac, he transcended the terrestrial categories of moral actions; he placed absolute faith in the superiority of God's directives over relativistic human conceptions of reasonableness and rightness. Abraham's individual obedience transformed conduct ordinarily conceived as demoniacal, absurd or morally repugnant, into a supremely commendable act of absolute faith in God. The idea of faith as a leap beyond immediate perception, moral judgment and knowledge, or a refuge into which man is driven by the 'latent melancholy of unendurable despair' is a constantly recurring theme in Kierkegaard's writings. And this Biblical story furnishes the crowning proof of the irrational, improbable nature of faith.

Kierkegaard's position is perfectly consistent if he maintains that the dictates of the human conscience are necessarily relative and fallible in relation to God's perfect directives. It is preeminently self-coherent and ultimately moral to trust the commands of an infinitely wise and benevolent being who has either complete knowledge of the good or is Himself identical with the absolute, eternal good. In the former case, man's unwavering obedience to God as the infallible perceiver and transmitter of the good is his best guarantee of remaining in touch with perfect goodness. In the latter metaphysical structure, man's absolute creaturely duty to God is one with an absolute moral duty to do the good. In both cases an individual's consistent adherence to God's commands assures him of unerring moral insights. We may grumble about the metaphysics of either system but we cannot question the internal coherence which results in the above consequences.

However, does Kierkegaard hold this view which has been

Deity and Morality

imputed to him? Although he does seem at times to be maintaining this type of position, e.g. when he speaks of Abraham's confidence that Isaac would be returned to him unharmed, I would say that the main tenor of his thought is significantly different. This difference can be pointed up by noticing a distinction which Kierkegaard explicitly defines. In an attempt to further characterize Abraham's situation Kierkegaard contrasts it with a purported incident of the Trojan War in which Agamemnon is told by the seer Calchas that the goddess demands his daughter Iphigenia as a sacrifice of expiation before the Greek fleet will be allowed to sail. Kierkegaard describes Agamemnon here as a *tragic hero* whereas Abraham is a *knight of faith*. 'The difference between the tragic hero and Abraham is clearly evident. The tragic hero still remains within the ethical. He lets one expression of the ethical find its *telos* in a higher expression of the ethical; . . . With Abraham the situation was different. By his act he over-stepped the ethical entirely and possessed a higher *telos* outside of it, in relation to which he suspended the former. . . . It was not for the sake of saving a people, not to maintain the idea of the state, that Abraham did this, and not in order to reconcile angry deities . . . the story of Abraham contains a teleological suspension of the ethical.'[9]

Here we see that the justification for Abraham's action is not faith in the ultimate moral wisdom and goodness of God's judgment but the Individual's personal relationship to God—a relationship of Creature to Creator, of absolute obedience to the authoritative pronouncement of God. This relationship of faith in which the individual 'stands naked before his Maker' furnishes the grounds for Abraham's dogmatic decision despite the fact that God's will is abstruse to the point of opaqueness, improbable to the point of irrationality and morally objectionable to the point of depravity. His decision is not just a strangling of temporal reason in the hope of grasping an eternal ethic, but a transcendence of ethics altogether. The absolute acceptance of the will of God is self-justifying and does not depend for its rightness upon second order assumptions concerning the relationship between God and morality, i.e. that God is identical with or possesses infinite knowledge of the good. 'This position cannot be mediated, for all mediation comes about precisely by virtue of the universal; it is and remains to all eternity a paradox, inaccessible to thought.'[10] This frequently reiterated point affirms that we are utterly precluded from bringing Abraham's action into relation with the universal.

Now where there is a conflict between the moral dictates of our human conscience and the commands of God it is one thing to obey God's will in the faith that thereby one is electing the ultimately moral course of action, but quite another to elect obedience on the assumption that duty to God supersedes or supplants moral considerations altogether. The latter is a much weaker position, for to resolve a contradiction by claiming that God's moral perception is superior to man's is on much firmer footing than maintaining that God's will overrides reason and ethics. In the one case we are plunged into a supra-rational, in the other an irrational; in the one case we are told that our decision has deep moral roots, in the other that moral considerations are irrelevant.

Furthermore, in the latter case (let us call it B) one has not any check on the validity of this metaphysical system other than the direct word of God[11] because it cannot be judged by criteria of reasonableness, moral appropriateness or any mediations of the universal, whereas in the former case (let us label it A) reason is a decidedly pertinent factor in our decision, in addition to the apprehension of God's wishes.

Totally irrationalistic theories are self-defeating; however, Kierkegaard's position (B) involves some rational assumptions and for this reason cannot be demolished on logical grounds. Although rationally deciding that we are justified in suspending a totally rational decision is a more rational procedure than deciding to proceed without any rational backing or in the face of rational considerations, both contain an element of the rational in the primary quasi-methodological decision. This is not Kierkegaard's point but a logical point. We have rationally decided upon the reference-grounds for our decision even though the decision itself may be irrational. It is a logically sound process to

Deity and Morality

decide rationally to be irrational, just as it is logically permissible to decide consistently in favour of inconsistent action of course. Difficulties may be encountered at the level of presenting reasons for being rational in the first instance but not in the second. It would be incumbent upon an individual adopting position (B) to find reasons for being rational in the first instance and irrational in the second, whereas a person embracing position (A) would have the relatively easier task of finding reasons for being rational in the first case and proceeding beyond the rational in the second. An attempt could be made to justify the apparent difficulties in both position (A) and (B) by reference to the revelation of God's will which made the irrational or supra-rational leap mandatory. For Kierkegaard does not maintain that God specifically instructed man to completely hold reason in abeyance, but he does claim that God tells us to perform unreasonable act, e.g. 'Take now thy son, thine only son Isaac, whom thou lovest, and get thee into the land of Moriah; and offer him there for a burnt-offering upon one of the mountains which I will tell thee of.'

However Kierkegaard's position, (B) is not only weaker than (A) by relying extremely heavily upon revelation for its sanctions, but is, I maintain, untenable for epistemological considerations concerning this supporting revelation.

To begin with, when we speak of an individual standing immediately before God and receiving a divine revelation of His will, particularly when we claim that deity has availed Himself of human speech to make His commands known as in the case of Abraham and other instances of verbal inspiration mentioned in the Bible, we must always remember that these perceptions have necessarily been channelled through one or more of our senses. Whether we say that the individual concerned has received a revelation which is public and general or private and esoteric, this revelation occurs to finite individuals located in space and time; it is legitimate, therefore, to regard it as a message mediated through our sense of hearing or seeing.

It has been argued that exceptions to this general rule are revelations of God's purpose in nature and history, e.g. the Hebrew conceptions of divine providence arising from contemplation of nature and a sense of divine protection.[12] However, although it might be strongly argued that these are revelations of God's will in the sense of signs by means of which God has historically indicated righteous pathways or left conspicuous traces of His handiwork (as cosmological and teleological *proofs* maintain) they are not revelations in Kierkegaard's sense of direct, divinely inspired messages. Therefore, although it might prove interesting to analyse the way in which historical events or the construction of the world are perceived revelations, we need not concern ourselves to do so.

Since all immediacy of the sort Kierkegaard deals with is filtered through our senses, the belief that we have an absolute duty to obey the voice of God must also mean that we have an absolute duty to trust dictates transmitted through our faculties—to have complete faith in the infallibility of our senses to transmit authentic revelations. Kierkegaard would preclude us from questioning the validity of a claim mediated through relatively unreliable means on the grounds that *the claim*, God's will, must be unquestionably accepted on faith. The stress which Kierkegaard places on the absolute duty which man owes to his Creator would exclude our assessing, our hearing (and understanding) of the Absolute voice, on the supposition that we are doubting the wisdom of God's commands. But surely this need not be so. Doubting that a command was issued by God on epistemological grounds does not mean doubting the omniscience of deity or the absolute duty which man owes to God. Although we must entertain a high degree of confidence concerning the reliability of our faculties as a presupposition of knowledge, it is precisely at a moment of paradox such as Kierkegaard alludes to that the witness of our senses must be rigorously examined—when one believes to have heard the voice of God saying, 'Kill your son'. Surely this is not the moment for absolute obedience but for extreme caution. It is at this moment that the dangerous subjectivity of private revelation becomes apparent, and in order to avoid a misguided dogmatism or an insulated eccentricity we must question our ability to reliably discern a revelation of God's will. It is only after we are thoroughly convinced of the authenticity of a revelation, i.e. that a particular revelation has in fact been made by God, that we are (perhaps) justified in acting upon it. (Whether this is a sufficient condition for action or merely a necessary condition is a crucial dilemma as we shall see.)

I said, above, that to doubt on epistemological grounds that a command was issued by God does not entail doubting the supreme wisdom of deity. I should like to elaborate upon this sentence and say that it is quite the contrary in our experience of revelation. Our belief in the superlative nature of God forces us to doubt the validity of the evidence transmitted by our senses. This is my second point. When we doubt that God issued a command we usually do so on moral and/or theological grounds as well as epistemological grounds—the sort of touchstone which Kierkegaard would also disallow by his definition of faith. When individuals reject the authenticity of a revelation it is as much on the grounds that God would not issue such a command as it is that our sense perception has malfunctioned. In most cases, in fact, the reliability of our senses and the authenticity of a revelation is disputed in the first instance on moral/theological grounds. We usually say, 'Our knowledge of God's nature achieved, for example, through the teachings of Jesus, indicates that "kill thy neighbour and thyself" cannot be a true revelation of His will. Therefore, it did not proceed from God and our senses have proved unreliable in persuading us that it did.' Although the direction from which our knowledge of God issues remains that of Creator-to-creature, a salutary moral, theological and epistemological check is maintained on the authenticity of utterances attributed to God. Kierkegaard's system would not exert any controls over a self-convinced bigot, deviant, or fanatic.

In emphasizing that revelations must be judged in the light of moral judgments, theological doctrine and epistemological considerations, we need not go as far as Catholicism does and proclaim that our revelation 'should be submitted to the opinion of a prudent priest' before we allow it 'pious credence', but at the same time we cannot carry Protestant individuality to the point of absurdity as Kierkegaard would have us do. And Kierkegaard's individualism cannot evade the charge of idiosyncratic subjectivism by saying it is *the Individual naked before God* or the Individual in relation to the Absolute rather than privately manufacturing truths, if he will not consider public interpretations of God's will or the judgments of conscience or reason itself to count against his conception of the divine voice.[13]

I might add in this connection that Kierkegaard uses a Biblical example to epitomize his point; however, the primary function of Biblical criticism (particularly Higher Criticism) is to apply critical, scientific tests of philology, archaeology and history to each of the books composing the Bible in order to separate true revelations of God's will from the myths, legends and strictly human productions deeply rooted in the time and circumstances of their compilation. In addition to these scientific criteria of authenticity, if man's conscience condemns the acts reported and justified in the name of God's revelation, then we dismiss these passages as apocryphal on moral grounds or re-interpret them according to contemporary conceptions of the moral nature of deity. (Whether one judges an individual reprehensible for committing unjust or cruel actions with the unselfish motives of obeying God's will depends upon one's moral viewpoint. Intentionalists would absolve him of blame, teleologists would condemn him.)

A more philosophically interesting dilemma which Kierkegaard does not pose is one in which a private revelation is received which is morally abhorrent yet the epistemological under-structure of which survives stringent scrutiny. That is to say, a thorough questioning of the sense perception involved in the reception of a divine revelation fails to reveal significant doubts as to its validity and hence the genuine nature of the sense data. Kierkegaard's paradox centres upon a creature's absolute obedience to God's commands even when these commands are morally repugnant. We can slip through the horns of this dilemma by questioning the reliability of our auditory and visual senses—by showing that our absolute duty may be to obey the true voice of God but it surely is not to place absolute faith in the witness of our senses. However, when doubt as to the validity of our senses has been satisfied and we unreservedly declare that a bad command issued by God is a genuine command of God, then we are thrown into a neat dilemma indeed. When a real or theoretical schism of this basic sort occurs we cannot straddle it by saying that we are morally right in doing what our conscience dictates and religiously justified in obeying deity. This 'solution' does not resolve the issue but renders it all the more tortuous when we are eventually faced with deciding which course of action man ought to follow. It seems a sound assumption to many that if God in fact wills what is wrong we ought to disobey the will of God. This position opts for the supremacy of moral judgment to religious obedience; it proceeds on the assumption that God's commands must be judged worthy of obedience, i.e. morally right, before obedience is justified.

NOTES

Chapter III

1. I have taken the remarks which Hume makes in explicitly discussing his theological position, that God does not influence man, to mean that he does not issue any sort of directives—particularly not moral directives. However, the logical conclusion of his paragraph on *ought* and *is* in the *Enquiry*, is that even if God did utter moral pronouncements or injunctions, this alone would not be sufficient to assure as that these commands were right. Thus according to the laws of inference, neither God's commanding X nor His not commanding X entails that X is either right or wrong.
2. Nielsen, Kai, 'Some Remarks on the Independence of Morality From Religion', *Mind*, Vol. LXX, No. 278, April 1961, p. 175.
3. *The Dialogues of Plato*, trans. by B. Jowett, Oxford, 1953, Vol. I, p. 318.
4. Heidel, W. A., *Plato's Euthyphro*, London, D. Appleton & Co., 1902, p. 17.
5. *Euthyphro* trans. by H. N. Fowler, London, Wm Heinemann, 1914, p. 41.
6. *The Dialogues of Plato*, p. 139.
7. Dennes, Wm R., 'Knowledge and Values' in *Symbols and Values*, ed. by L. Bryson, New York, Harper & Bros., 1954, p. 605.
8. Murray, A. V., *Natural Religion and Christian Theology*, London, James Nisbet & Co., Ltd, 1956, p. 47 and p. 43.
9. Kierkegaard, A., *Fear and Trembling*, trans. by W. Lowrie, Princeton, Princeton University Press, 1941, pp. 79-88.
10. Kierkegaard, A., *ibid.*, p. 82.

11. This may appear a sufficient condition for an action; however epistemological considerations render it far less certain than it seems as we will later show.
12. The doctrine that God has singled out the Jews for shepherdly protection could only be generated by an over-emphasis on relatively rare historical moments of deliverance.
13. For an excellent article on this subject see Packer, J. I., 'The Bible and the Authority of Reason', *The Churchman*, Vol. LXXV, No. 4, December 1961.

Chapter IV
DEITY AND MORALITY

A: MEDIAEVAL ATTITUDES

A number of different objections, both ancient and modern, have been made against the validity of this point. When theologians of the Middle Ages were obliged to discuss certain philosophical problems originating in theological controversies, e.g. problems of free will, the 'first' movement of sensibility (*primus motus*) and the notions of substance, person and hypostasis,[1] they were also faced, as Burnet points out, with this problem of *Whether an act is right because God loves it, or whether God loves it because it is right.* Since a conclusion in favour of the latter alternative would entail the supremacy of the moral order and human judgment, the Christian apologists of the day approached it as a foreign, insidious disease to be quickly stamped out. This was not because they were, by current standards, closed-minded, dogmatic and arrogant, but because of their unquestioned, inherited conviction that when reason and faith conflicted, reason was necessarily in error.[2] Reason *seemed to* lead to the irresistible conclusion that morality held the primary position in the universe, but we *knew* from knowledge of Scripture that God was sovereign.

The reason for this extraordinary set of attitudes has its roots deep in the soil of scholastic thinking. For mediaeval theologians (which class includes all the great mediaeval minds prior to the Renaissance) regarded the dogmatic teaching of the Church as permanent and inelastic. Human reason, corrupted in the sin of Adam, must abdicate when its judgments, or worse still, the results of its investigations, conflicted with Revelation. Man's intellect being in a state of permanent corruption was unable to fathom the purity and depth of God's being. Therefore unreasoned acceptance of the literal accuracy of Scripture, and synthesis of various sacred writings (through grace and faith) was the only means toward achieving any accurate knowledge of God.[3]

Drawing upon Paul's advice to the Colossians, 'Beware lest any man spoil you through philosophy and vain deceit',[4] the mediaeval theologian remained secure in an impregnable citadel. Tertullian is representative of the attitude of the day when he states, 'We want no curious disputation after possessing Jesus Christ, no inquisition after enjoying the Gospel. When we believe (*credimus*), we desire nothing beyond it to believe (*credere*).'[5] Verbal paradoxes such as the one with which we are concerned were therefore of no substantive relevance to the esoteric, self-sustaining theology. Reason has here led to a *cul de sac*, an affirmation of the primacy of human assessment and the moral order over God's supreme power. What better proof was there that philosophy readily turns into sophistry when unchecked by faith?

This widely held viewpoint should now be nothing more than an historical curiosity, a showpiece of archaic thought. Unfortunately, it is still quite prevalent, notably among Barthian Protestants. However, the alarming question did arise at that time among theologians as to how one can select from among the divergent interpretations of the Christian Revelation, which account possessed God's truth, except by human judgment of the insights claimed by each protagonist. It helped little to say God pointed the way because it still remained for human beings to discern the direction in which He was pointing. Personal insight was ultimately required to discern truth not authoritative declarations. As F. R. Tennant has said, 'unless theological and religious truth is thus found, personally discerned and appropriated, it scarcely is truth *for us*, i.e. of spiritual value to us. So the Reformation and the Enlightenment taught us for all time; and had the discovery been made and assimilated in the early days of dogmatic theology, the history, and much of the structure, of ecclesiastical doctrine, as also the institutional embodiment of doctrine, would doubtless have been different.'[6]

Deity and Morality

The conspicuous (and increasing) lack of unanimity in the Mediaeval Christian world as to the direction served to thrust home the vital nature of the issue. And an even more embarrassing question for Christendom was how one could justifiably choose, from among the revelations embodiment in the sacred writings of various religions of the world, which account of God's nature and duties we ought to accept, except by a human assessment of their respective merits. What would have happened to the dynamic evolution of man's conception of God if mankind had frozen its understanding at a lower level than that *zenith* achieved in the Middle Ages? By adopting the same sort of blind loyalty to revelation, the development of religious truth might well have progressed no further than a deification of the sky or some large and remote object like the sun, or an animistic personification of the mysteries or forces of nature, or the worship of a mythical ancestor. Sin would have consisted only in the neglect of some rite or ceremony, acts of prayer would have functioned only to appease the wrath of malicious spirits, religious objects would be possessed of magical properties, and the deity would be sought in the uncanny or mysterious happenings of life. The very fact that mankind has progressed beyond these infantile conceptions of religion, shows that human beings have assessed their revelations in the light of reason, and judged certain of them to be the 'lispings of infantile humanity'.

The supremacy of human judgment cannot be usurped in controversies among Christian believers or between Christians and others, by saying that if we, or the sanctified fathers of our religion, were overwhelmingly convinced by a revelatory experience, then we cannot retrospectively question its validity. For the uncivilized inhabitants of Fiji, Australia, Siberia, Africa, etc., were no less convinced of the truth of their revelations than the Christian Schoolmen were of theirs. This is very like the argument from conceivability all over again. To make matters still worse, some of the most hideous and reprehensible human actions have been performed by individuals who were sincerely convinced than an overwhelming revelation of God's will directed their steps. Witness the witch hunts in Salem, Massachusetts, the Spanish Inquisition, the cult of stranglers in Bombay, the human sacrifices offered by Guatamalan natives, the murders of the Reformation, etc.

Numerous atrocities can also be said to result from human judgment (unless one holds that, by definition, whenever terribly cruel actions are performed deliberative judgment has been held in abeyance) but it seems a more reliable method of gaining knowledge and avoiding the pitfalls associated with fanaticism. It has the meritorious characteristic of being theoretically open to criticism from any quarter. In addition, it can claim to its credit such things as that every position can be examined for logical difficulties, the value of different viewpoints can be reasonably weighed in the light of common criteria, and empirical foundations or references can be checked for accuracy. None of this can be said for arguments conducted in the shadow of an incontestable revelation—usually with the disputants quaking under the tyranny of heresy indictments. Too often a thoroughgoing reliance upon revelation is an inviolable method of guaranteeing the truth of some otherwise undemonstrable point. Since by the very nature of its epistemological position it is private and unconfirmable by ordinary empirical standards, appeals to revelation readily degenerate into a desperate expedient.

There is one counter-argument which Apologists might put forward which seems to me to have some merit. The person in possession of a revelation such as those major pronouncements of Scripture; or even that which is contained in Scripture is indubitable, might defend his claims as follows: After epistemological objections have failed to render his claim untenable (Cf. Kierkegaard discussion, Ch. 3), he might declare that the nature of the experience which he has undergone is simply not amenable to confirmation by ordinary methods, and then go on to bemoan this fact, possessing such certainty of the truth of his revelation that he ardently desires to present proof to the leagues of doubters on their own grounds. However, assuming he is sincere, and thoroughly convinced of the exclusive character of his revelation,

Deity and Morality

he will refuse to be untrue to his experience by saying it is rationalistic rather than legalistic and therefore open to ordinary confirmation. He would make the same claims whether this position was favourable or unfavourable to the credibility of his conclusions. In this case the consequences of the nature of the experience happen in one sense to be favourable, for it is thereby placed beyond conventional criticism.

As a comparable case one might cite the philosopher's objection to concluding the actual existence of God from human *desires* that He exist. The results of a Christian God possessing ontological status would certainly be emotionally satisfying, e.g. we would have an omnipotent being to intervene on our behalf in answer to prayers, we would upon commitment to various tenets, be guaranteed eternal life, we would have firmly codified laws of moral conduct, we would be assured of just desserts being meted out in the next world to the unscrupulous but powerful entrepreneurs, politicians, and opportunists of this world. But the existence of God is not a fact for these desirable consequences; the wish does not imply an objective reality, as every spinster will tell you whose marriage hopes have remained unfulfilled,[7] and every psychologist will tell you who is acquainted with the twisted thinking arising from wish-fulfilment desires.

Similarly, although the man in possession of a self-convincing revelation may wish that the accuracy of his experience was testable by the usual empirical validating methods, he cannot claim that it is. Yet like the poet, painter and composer, he uses a particular medium because the special reality which he is trying to capture is best captured in this form. Perhaps the artists' insights are somewhat translatable into conceptual language as the critic attempts to do, but his theme is best expressed, that is most fully and adequately expressed, in the forms which the artists have chosen for them. It is far more probable that artists do not write essays to convey the subject-matter which preoccupies them because they find this form unsuitable or inadequate, than that they are illiterate, inarticulate or even unadept at reasonable expression. A sequence of notes, a poetic image, or a brush stroke is found to be more deeply eloquent to express the profundities which the artist feels he has glimpsed, than any syllogistic formulation.

In the same way the revelationist will be convinced that the essence of his subject-matter, God in this instance, is most fully grasped (or perhaps can only be grasped), by means of the medium of revelation. No matter how much pressure is exerted upon him in the form of stressing the epistemological and methodological difficulties inherent in his stand, he will not claim that the concept of God of His attributes bears formulation in straightforward, ordinary terms. To assert this mode of reality to his revelation would be to perjure himself before the Holy Spirit. What he will insist upon, however, is that his experience be given space alongside of other types of experience that happen (*ex hypothesi*) to be more easily verifiable. He will ask that we do not allow ourselves to be pragmatically prejudiced in favour of, for example, the more 'scientifically' desirable experiences—i.e. those that can be scrutinized in test tubes, analysed in truth tables, dissected under microscopes, inscribed in historical documents, recorded on statistical charts or even determined dialectically. He will fume and rant about revelation being of such a private nature that it often nourishes an obscurantist dogmatism or infallibilism, that it sanctifies the utterances of the crank or bigot no less than the prophet and offers spurious justification for atrocities, even after epistemological considerations have eliminated certain undesirables; but he will demand with equal vehemence that his revelation be not discredited out of hand and thrown out of court because it fails to exhibit characteristics which it necessarily does not possess. This would be the negative version of the naturalistic fallacy in reverse. It is denying a claim as to what *is* on the basis of what the consequences *ought* not to be!

A good deal can be said for the validity of this point of view. To my mind every objection against it merely emphasizes the utility and facility-of-handling of the underpinnings of other types of theories, and the tremendous risks of self-deception or deliberate falsification inherent in revelationary claims. Admittedly these are important considerations in themselves, but the utmost efficacy which such criticisms can have is to caution us to be more chary of revelation as a means of gaining knowledge than we need to be about human experiences which are open to public verification; they cannot entirely dispense with this way of knowledge or the claims arising therefrom. Because the process is fallible it does not follow that the conclusion is necessarily untrue, any more than we can conclude complete human ignorance from our liability to error. We cannot pontificate that revelation is so unreliable that, in the interests of science, it ought to be excluded from serious consideration or relegated to a subservient position, for thereby we may be eliminating a mode of reality which does not lend itself to expression in any other form. However deep our personal distaste for this *tour de force*, it might well be something for which we should perhaps be thankful—some would say, thankful to God.

B: CONTEMPORARY THOUGHT

To return to our main point, since the power of the Schoolmen's objection to Plato's conclusion that *God loves an act because it is right* emanated from their belief in the infinite epistemological superiority of the revelations of Scripture, once this belief was seriously doubted, the principal argument against the supremacy of human judgment and the *moral order* was likewise undermined. If the accuracy of the method of revelation had remained unquestionable, so would the utter sovereignty of God; however, as suspicions about the former grew in the Mediaeval mind, distrust of the latter also developed. A one to one correspondence does not logically exist between the cause and its effect (or rather the reason and its consequences), but doubt concerning the infallibility of revelational *evidence* was a sufficient reason in this context for doubting God's supreme authority.[8]

Another avenue of attack is that of regarding this issue as but another example of the staggering difficulties which have been thrust in the path of modern theological discourse.

It was a great blow to man's religious security for Copernicus to prove the universe heliocentric rather than geocentric, and for

Deity and Morality

nineteenth-century Darwinism to interpret human life as having evolved, by a gradual yet continual process, from the earliest forms of living organisms—amoebic specks of protoplasmic jelly in the scum of tides. (It was also a deadly blow to man's spiritual pride, for until these revolutionary findings became known, the Hebraic notion of the *chosen people* had not been abandoned, but merely enlarged to include all of mankind.) However, these conflicts arose out of head-on contradictions between the dogmatic beliefs of religion and the pronouncements of science.

Recently the assertions of religion have been weathering an oblique attack as new criticisms held them to be not false but intrinsically meaningless. More specifically, since the heyday of the Verification Principle when a thoroughgoing empiricism shook the foundations of that bulk of theological and metaphysical assertions which could not be confirmed (or discredited) by empirical evidence,[9] religious language has been plagued with linguistic difficulties of one sort or another. Even after the Vienna Circle had abandoned its youthfully exuberant and brutish deification of verifiability and confirmability, recognizing that they were excluding by empirical presuppositions (functioning as *definitional jokers*[10]) an extravagant number of meaningful utterances and propositions, theologians remained justifiably self-conscious and chary about their utterances.

For example, questions such as *Does there exist a God?* and *Is there a God?* have replaced the formulations of the same central issue in terms of *Does God exist?* and *Is God a real existent?* For *Does God exist?* was found to apply existence to a proper name, and *Is God a real existent?* confused *exist* and *real*.[11] Using similar methods of criticism, the statement, *There is a God*, was carefully scrutinized in order to determine if *There is* . . . was being used in a literal, straightforward sense, as in *There are kangaroos*. If one concluded that it was being used as an empirical assertion, all sorts of problems concerning the *cash value* of this sentence immediately presented themselves.

A goodly core of theologians have answered the above question in the negative, saying that this vital component of religious discourse is significantly unlike any statement referring to objects of experience. Since God is a unique, transcendent being, sentences containing the word *God*, whether they function as moral exhortation, an expression of worship, dedication, or an alleged historical fact, are necessarily excluded from being placed on equal footing with sentences of a *terrestrial* nature, much less sentences that can readily be given appropriate *cash value*.[12] Although we must predicate of God, who *ex hypothesi* transcends the finite and temporal, qualities which are derived from finite and temporal experience, we must avoid characterizing him in sentences offering a literal identification with such experience. In fact, if sentences containing the word *God* were essentially like such empirical assertions, then we would be justified in regarding the deity to which they refer as an unfit object of worship and veneration.[13]

Judging that the same sort of problem in theological discourse is present in discussing divine commands, the theologian will respond to the dilemma previously described in an identical manner. He will hold that *God wills X* is essentially different from X_1 *wills* X_2 when X_1 is anything but a strict synonym for God. This becomes abundantly clear when we appreciate the full logic of the word *God*.

We cannot legitimately place *Christopher Wren wills X* and *God wills X* in the same class; the former is an architect, the latter the *Master Architect*. We cannot place *John Osborne wills X* and *God wills X* on equal footing, despite their syntactical similarity, for the one is an author, the other the *Supreme Author*. Similarly, although Hercules is reputedly powerful and Aristotle admittedly wise, we cannot treat *Hercules wills X* or *Aristotle wills X*, as being on all fours with *God wills X*, because of the essential difference that God is *All-Powerful* and *Omniscient*. God is not just another being or bit of metaphysical furniture, but a traditionally unique entity of the universe. To treat Him in the manner described above is to fail to do justice to this uniqueness. The analogical argument collapses because the comparative components are not alike in all essentials respects.

If we glance backwards into ecclesiastical history, particularly

Deity and Morality

into the theological positions of the Schoolmen, the dignity of this theme is enhanced by the discovery that God is traditionally regarded as a unique being, separate and distinct from the created order. When John Scotus Erigena in *De Divisione Naturae* classifies *Nature* into four aspects or stages of one world process, he never makes the pantheist's and modern philosopher's mistake of confusing God with these aspects of being; God remains the ultimate grounds of nature, a part of the universe yet underlying its essence, in all things yet transcending all things. Dionysius the Areopagite makes the paradoxical assertion that 'God is nothing' only because He defies and transcends all formulations and hence is inexpressible; so great is the gap between His nature and ours that even Scripture can only offer metaphor, analogy, and symbol—never direct insight. (See *Divine Names*.) In the metaphor of Duns Scotus which compares the universe to a magnificent tree, whose root is matter and whose trunk is split into two great physical and spiritual branches, God is not the bark, sap, fruit or flowers of the tree, but its planter and tender. (See *De Rerum Principio*.) William of Ockham's iconoclastic nominalism nevertheless clearly places God independent of all minds, orders and laws of reality, with the moral and physical fibre of the universe determined solely by the decisions of His external will. (See *Quodlibeta*.) The central doctrine of St Anselm's *Proslogium* and *Monologium* is that God is the exemplary, efficient and final cause of the sensible and intelligible world, necessarily lying wholly beyond and above it. St Thomas's concept (with heavy debts to Aristotle's *De Anima*) of a scale of existence, places God at the summit of the chain of being, and in a totally unique position as the only 'purely spiritual Being'. All of these thinkers relegate man to an inferior, separate and significantly different position than that occupied by God.

Now the modern theologian's pathway out of the maze constructed by logical considerations as to the strict necessity of human judgment prior to religious obedience is actually through a modern restatement of the same point. He will claim that since God occupies a wholly unique position in the metaphysical scheme, the standards of logic which are usually applied to

Deity and Morality

mandates of a conventional order, are rendered inoperative when focused upon Him. It would be like discounting the corollary of plane geometry that parallel lines never meet by applying the proof of solid geometry to it. Or to borrow Karl Heim's simile, it would be like switching on a light to see the nature of darkness.

Canon Ramsey fully dressed this point in contemporary clothing when he suggested to me in conversation that we cannot speak of God willing X and let us say the Prime Minister willing X in the same breath. For to do so would be to anthropomorphize God in a highly unacceptable way; it would be to place God, or rather demote Him to the same level as that occupied by any executive official. Once God is thus reduced in stature, so as to be one with the Prime Minister, Gandhi, Stalin or what have you, it is a relatively simple task to demonstrate that a human judgment as to the rightness of His orders is requisite for obedience to them. What we have done in order to depose God from His position of supremacy and erect Mammon in his place, is, in Ryle's famous phrase, to commit a *category-mistake*.

However the point is not so easily won. For once we have demonstrated that God is traditionally placed in a unique position in the metaphysical scheme, and also shown that as the holder of this position we have done Him the injustice of applying inappropriate, *foreign logic* to His commands, it still remains for us to describe the sort of logical structure that is peculiarly suited to His being. If this is another case of attempting to dissect a delicate biological organism with mechanic's tools, the onus is upon us to provide information about this unfamiliar specimen and to prescribe the kind of instrument to be employed in dealing with it. If our claim is that God is the only member of a superior and different class, in what way is this class or category unique? We have elliptically indicated the sort of entity that God is not; we must now declare what sort of creature. He is and in a sense *prove* what He is not. Otherwise, we have not refuted Plato's point that the acceptability of God's authority rests upon human judgement of the rightness of the action which He commands. The burden of proof being squarely placed on the affirmative in argumentation, we must show why it is that such criticisms are drained of relevance when applied to God, or else concede our point to be a vague hope, or worse, an insincere evasion.

For example, Professor Ryle first applied the label *category mistake* to treating *mind* as a *thing*—word, then proceeded to present an argument as to why a misclassification has occurred when one does so. He states[14] that if the word *mind* is regarded as a *thing*-word, it must refer, presumably to some recondite ghost-like *thing*, occupying and controlling bodily machinery. Then minds, if they existed at all, would be completely mysterious and unknown entities. Statements purporting to give information about people's minds would be *uncashable* and consequently meaningless. Therefore, to place the word *mind* on all fours with the word *body* would constitute a *category-mistake*, giving rise to unnecessary and bogus problems.

Now presumably, theologians who are concerned with establishing the nature of the category inhabited by God, would want to separate it from the realm of things—that is, the familiar, straightforward category of objects which have an empirical frame of reference.[15] Otherwise, one would be hard put to determine His colour, size, shape, texture and spatio-temporal position as one can readily do with, say, an automobile. If we attempted to squeeze *God* into some straightforward empirical category, He would also be judged as a recondite, mysterious entity, in fact the sort of creature that Flew's explorers set traps for around a jungle garden. (With such an empirical model as a gardener being employed for an analogical argument, it comes as no shock that God is disparagingly characterized as invisible, intangible, and eternally elusive by ordinary sense data.)[16]

It is also usually denied that God properly belongs in the category of necessary truths; that is, that theological propositions purporting to offer information about God are not of an analytical sort. For example, the proposition *All fathers have children* is analytic because its truth or falsity is discoverable through an analysis of the subject *fathers*. The predicate is actually superfluous to anyone who possesses a thorough understanding of the

Deity and Morality

subject, for the idea made explicit in the predicate was implicit (*a priori*) in the subject. However, in the case of theological propositions such as *God is good* two independent ideas are being linked together. Since God's attributes are established *a posteriori* by independent means, it is *logically possible* in the full technical sense of the phrase, that God could be discovered not to be good; but it would be grossly self-contradictory to declare that all (or even some) fathers do not have children. (If we could not think of God without thinking of His goodness, would we be giving testimony to a conditioned response, or making a metaphysical point?)

Then what sort of category is deity in? What sort of category does theological language (as distinct from general religious language) inhabit that it is legitimately enabled to transcend criticisms that would apply to it if its truth depended upon its empirical claims or its logical necessity? As I. M. Crombie states: 'It is said, the (theological) statements purport to be about a quasi-personal subject, and in that way to be parallel to statements about, say, Julius Caesar, and yet if we proceed to draw conclusions from them, to bring arguments against them, in general to test them as if they were parallel to statements about Julius Caesar, we are told that we have failed to grasp their function. They have, apparently, some kind of special exemption from empirical testing; and yet if one attempts, for this reason, to assimilate them to other kinds of utterances (moral judgments for example, or mathematical formulae) which enjoy similar exemption, one is at once forbidden to do so.'[17]

NOTES

Chapter IV

1. DE WULF, M., *History of Mediaeval Philosophy*, trans. by E. C. Messenger, London, Thomas Nelson and Sons Ltd., 1951, Vol. II, p. 281.
2. Mediaeval theologians also refused to look through Galileo's telescope for fear that they might be convinced by the unreliable evidence of their senses of something which they *knew* from Revelation was untrue.
3. Some theologians of the period thought that complete reliance upon

Scripture was sufficient, philosophical demonstrations actually diminishing the merit of faith. Others regarded *rational faith* as possessing greater value than unsupported belief. And a third faction weighed *simple faith* and philosophical *rationalization* equally. All groups were agreed, however, that since Revelation through Scripture was infallible, at no moment could reason contradict faith. If reason and faith collided, so much the worse for reason.

4. Col. ii. 8.
5. Wolfson, H. A., *The Philosophy of the Church Fathers*, Cambridge, Mass., Harvard University Press, 1956, p. 102.
6. Tennant, F. R., *Philosophical Theology*, Cambridge, 1956, Vol. II, p. 226.
7. I owe this example to Montefiore, A., *A Modern Introduction to Moral Philosophy*, London, Routledge & Kegan Paul, 1958.
8. This is a logical point not an historical one, although historical knowledge is necessary for its comprehension. I might add that the converse is also true but for different reasons.
9. For outstanding studies of the historical development of this movement consult Morris, C. W., *Logical Positivism, Pragmatism and Scientific Empiricism*, Paris, Herman et Cie., 1937; Nagel, E., 'Impressions and Appraisals of Analytic Philosophy in Europe' in *Logic Without Metaphysics*, Glencoe, Illinois, The Free Press, 1956; Neurath, O., *Le Developpement du Cercle de Vienne*, Paris, Hermann et cie., 1935.
10. See Flew, A. G. N., 'The Justification of Punishment', *Philosophy*, Vol. XXIX, No. 111, October 1954, p. 292.
11. For an examination of this last point consult Austin, J. L., 'Other Minds', Aristotelian Society Supplementary Volume XX, 1946, p. 159.
12. Professor Ramsen's broad conclusion (in his book *Religious Languages*, London, A. C. M. Press, 1957, p. 49) is 'that if a rather strange discernment-commitment is the kind of situation characteristic of religion, we must expect religious language to be appropriately odd, and to have a distinctive logical behaviour.'
13. This dilemma, with apologies to Archibald MacLeish, might be phrased: If God is God He is not known, if God is known He is not God; take the even, take the odd.
14. Ryle, F., *The Concept of Mind*, London, Hutchinson, 1949, Ch. I.
15. Although H. D. Lewis seems at times to be saying that God must stand the test of truth or falsity in the normal sense of these words, his main characterization of religious experience implicitly denies this claim. He states at one point that religious experiences have this peculiarity 'that while they remain in themselves finite throughout, that is have a content only appropriate to finite beings like ourselves, yet they can be seen to have also a reference beyond that; and, in their patterns and ramifications in experience as a whole, they afford us the clue we need to the way the un-

conditional reality on which we are dependent enters into special relations with us. . . .' (Lewis, H. D., *Our Experiences of God*, London, Allen & Unwin Ltd., 1959.) The *reference beyond that* and *clue* which ordinary experience offers us is the religiously important part of such experience, and clearly indicates that as a means to the achievement of other knowledge spiritually transcending itself, it is not one with ordinary sense data as it is usually handled in, for example, inductive generalizations.

16. Flew, A., 'Theology and Falsification', in *New Essays in Philosophical Theology*, ed. by A. Flew and A. Macintyre, London, S. C. M. Press, Ltd., 1955, p. 96.
17. Crombie, I. M., 'The Possibility of Theological statements', in *Faith and Logic*, ed. by Basil Mitchell, London, Allen & Unwin, Ltd, 1957, p. 33.

Chapter V

THE DOCTRINE OF INEFFABILITY

A: MYSTICAL KNOWLEDGE

One way in which the essential nature of religious utterances has been characterized is in terms of an attempted expression of the inexpressible. Religious discourse, it is maintained, is absurd and nonsensical precisely because theologians have mistakenly and misguidedly sought to translate religious experience into rational terms. Divine fiats such as *God wills X*, or other theological formulations belong in the class of *the unutterable*, and as members of this class, necessarily cannot be equated with any meaningful utterance, let alone one possessing literal meaning such as *the premier wills X*. These propositions cannot be understood by a penetrating analysis of their deeper meaning, for by the very nature of their exalted reference, they are necessarily precluded from making sense on any linguistic level. Neither can we redeem the meaningfulness of religious assertions by reference to more sophisticated standards than those applied to straightforward empirical assertions, for, by definition, there is not any *philosopher's stone* which can transform expressions referring to an inexpressible reality into a meaningful form.

Many mystics seem to be maintaining a position of this sort. With this standpoint in mind we have Butler saying 'Some mystics are of a metaphysical turn of mind and have endeavoured to give utterance to the thoughts their experiences have inspired. . . . But such speculations are (not) guaranteed by the mystic state in which they were conceived, are (not) to be identified with mysticism. . . .'[1] David Knowles in defining traditional mystical theology states as a characteristic of the mystical experience that it 'is wholly incommunicable, save as a bare statement, and in this respect all the utterances of the mystics are entirely inadequate as representations of the mystical experience, but it brings absolute certainty to the mind of the recipient'.[2] And finally, William James declares ineffability to be the handiest of his four marks in classifying the mystical state. 'The subject of it immediately says that it defies expression, that no adequate report of its contents can be given in words . . . its quality must be directly experienced; it cannot be imparted or transferred to others.'[3]

Now although mystics frequently assert that their experiences are not linguistically translatable, this claim is hardly consistent with their behaviour. Most mystics are, in fact, noted for their exuberant verbal effusion; they continually present prolix descriptions of their indescribable, unutterable experience. And at every turn we find mystics employing expressions like 'deep yet dazzling darkness', the 'embrace of the Beloved', the 'Cloud of Unknowing', a 'Divine Dark', etc., to characterize the transcendent experiences of mystical contemplation. In short, they translate that which they say is untranslatable, describe the indescribable, and express the inexpressible (albeit in an odd way).

A typical example of this type of mystical claim not in keeping with mystical practice occurs in the writings of Tennyson. In the *Life of Tennyson* (Vol. I, p. 320), the poet speaks of a 'kind of waking trance' induced by repeating his own name, 'till all at once, out of the intensity of the consciousness of individuality, the individual itself seemed to dissolve and fade away into boundless being: and this is not a confused state, but the clearest of the clearest, and the surest of the surest, the weirdest of the weirdest, utterly beyond words. . . .' However, this mystical monism in which the unity and solidarity of the universe is deeply felt but is 'beyond words' is not only well described in this autobiographical fragment, but also in the poem *The Ancient Sage*. Witness the following extract:

> 'And more, my son! for more than once when I
> Sat all alone, revolving in myself
> The word that is the symbol of myself

The Doctrine of Ineffability

> The mortal limit of the Self was loosed
> And past into the Nameless as a cloud
> Melts into Heaven. I touch'd my limbs, the limbs
> Were strange not mine—and yet no shade of doubt,
> But utter clearness, and thro' loss of Self
> The gain of such large life as match'd with ours
> Were Sun to Spark—unshadowable in words,
> Themselves but shadows of a shadow-world.'[4]

And although we are acquainted with the aphorisms of Confucius from the reports of his disciples in the *Li-ki* and he is said to have personally written the *Ch'un-ts'in*, nevertheless he professes to be silent about the divine, preferring to imitate what he called the silence of God. When pressed to speak he said, 'Does heaven speak? The four seasons pursue their courses, and all things are continually being produced, but does Heaven say anything?'

From these apparently flagrant inconsistencies we can gather that most mystics do not literally mean that the beatific state which has overwhelmed them cannot be expressed. Their real meaning seems to be that it cannot be directly expressed in a purely rational way, or that it cannot be understood on the ordinary linguistic level. Some mystics cannot directly describe their experiences yet desperately desire to communicate them; they employ symbolic language to suggest the exalted vision which they have witnessed. Numerous misconceptions have arisen from a failure on the part of critics to fully comprehend that mystical utterances are symbolic, allusive and oblique; that they can only hint at an abstruse mystery because this mystery, *qua* mystery, is not amenable to straightforward, detailed description. (As I. M. Crombie once remarked, it is foolish to demand the detailed anatomy of a mystery.)

All religion, of course, insofar as it lays Barthian stress upon the transcendence of deity, is forced to use symbols and figurative terms. Symbolism provides partial knowledge of a reality which eludes direct verbal expression and exposition. However, to mysticism, symbols are absolutely basic and essential as representations of a deeper reality directly encountered at privileged moments, as well as being a vehicle for rendering mystical experiences partially intelligible to less fortunate outsiders. Stutfield is so conscious of mysticism's preoccupation with the 'Vast Unknown', the tremendous depth of reality beyond our apprehension and only amenable to symbolic expression, that he believes 'a splendid and fundamental agnosticism' lies at the centre of all mysticism.[5] Most writers on mysticism, in fact, have recognized the immensely important role of symbolism although few have drawn Stutfield's conclusions. Evelyn Underhill devotes a chapter of her book to the various symbols employed by mystics,[6] while Récéjac spends nearly half of his book on this topic.[7] Miss E. Gregory regards symbolism as a principal feature of mysticism[8] while R. L. Nettleship defines mysticism as 'the belief that everything in being what it is, is symbolic of something more'.[9] There is a certain ambiguity, of course, in the meaning of *symbol* being used by these writers. In one sense it is an indirect linguistic vehicle for the expression of a transcendent reality; in the other it means that the objects of experience themselves, even sublime visions, are symbolic of a reality lying behind them. However, mystics either employ the term *symbol* in both of its senses or achieve a syncretization of them. For example, when Francisco de Osuna refers to the body as a box tightly enclosing the soul, *box* is used metaphorically in both senses while body in only a physical not a verbal symbol.

In the light of this analysis of the usual mystic's meaning of inexpressible, i.e. as incapable of straightforward, ordinary expression, we can see the point of Macintyre's observation that for the mystic 'such expressions as the unutterable take on an idiomatic sense in which they are of great use in describing and naming what they have experienced'.[10] Surely this is Tennyson's rhetorical meaning when he uses the phrase 'beyond words' alongside of superlatives, like 'weirdest', 'surest', and 'clearest'. 'Beyond words' is used to describe an experience just as 'nothingness' might do, even though it is usually taken as the absence of sensation, thought or experience.

Thus we see that most mystics cannot really do without

The Doctrine of Ineffability

symbols, images, rhythmic language and metaphors even though this mode of expression is disclaimed by rational theologians and deemed inadequate to convey his own transcendental vision. For if the mystic is to communicate his experience at all, if he is to stimulate the latent intuition of the uninitiated to divine heights, he must employ poetic language which by symbolism and imagery hints at something beyond a surface sense. Fundamentally then a mystic's experience is unformulable in the sense that in order to communicate it he is confined to poetic metaphor. We need not concern ourselves at this point over whether mystical expressions such as 'the Incomprehensible Light, enfolding us and penetrating us' have any cognitive content or whether they merely conjure up vague, visual images. What is pertinent here is the characterization of mystical utterances as logically akin to indirect, affective expressions.[11] This rendering of religious language can then be subsumed under poetic language, when we examine the relationship between poetic and religious utterances.

Some mystics, of course, do claim that their experiences are inexpressible without employing this phrase in an idiomatic sense. They actually criticize other mystics for attempting expression even in symbolic, poetic terms and fall silent when asked to describe their own experience. For example, the *Sama-Veda* asserts the *unknowable* and Herbert Spencer speaks of substance as unknowable. Obviously what is unknowable is unutterable. The Zen Buddhists continually stress the futility of verbal truth and the Zen master teaches by devices such as slaps designed to promote a sudden awakening.[12] For them discourse concerning essential reality is truly a mistaken attempt to utter the ineffable. We might twist Wittgenstein's utterance (*Tractatus* 6.522) and say that there is indeed the mystical; it is the inexpressible.

As far as I can determine, the notion of an unutterable experience of mystical contemplation has its root in one or all of three sources. First, there is its derivation from that aspect of mystical practice commonly called Quietism. This fundamentally means an immense spiritual quiescence cultivated as a condition of intense receptivity to (or recollection of, as in Bernardino de Laredo), the divine voice. Underhill pejoratively calls this 'the danger zone of introversion', and Ruysbroeck denounces it as 'treason towards God', however both fail to fully appreciate the nature of Quietism. For it is an active, ardent searching for God, a 'busy rest' rather than a sterile, passive relaxation of effort, and as such, forms an integral part of all mystical life.

However, it is all too easy to drift into a doctrine of silence concerning the knowledge achieved by this method. The Spanish mystic Francisco de Osuna demonstrates this tendency when he writes of his 'second way of silence' that the quiet hearer is 'silent to all around'. It can remain an untainted receptive Quietism as in Juan de Angeles[13] and the silent corporate fellowship of the Society of Friends; however, the epistemological necessity for silence in receiving a message, easily slides into the metaphysical impossibility of transmitting a message.

A second apparent source for the inexpressibility of divine mystical experience lies in the strong mystical tendency towards anti-intellectualism. It seems a recurrent strain in many thinkers such as Hocking,[14] Underhill,[15] Pratt,[16] Cordelier,[17] Sebatier, Höffding, Leuba and Pfeiderer to depreciate the ability of rational thought to reach reality. The intellect, we are reminded, classifies, sifts, unifies, constructs, co-ordinates, tabulates and explains the experience furnished to it; this 'careful mosaic of neatly-fitted conceptions which those intellects will offer us in return will have none of the peculiar qualities of life: it will be but a *practical simplification of reality*, made by the well-trained sorting-machine in the interests of our daily needs.'[18] It is through action of the will and emotional experience (particularly mystical impressions) that man is able to achieve life insights, to come in contact with naked reality. Miss Underhill repeatedly contrasts the 'static helplessness' of thought with the 'life movement' of intuitional experience. Reflective reason is for her (as for Lotze, Sartre, and perhaps even Bergson) a clumsy and remote instrument necessarily consigned to second-order issues. To 'feel the pulsations of (life's) mighty rhythm', to gain intuitive insights we need the help of artists, poets, prophets and seers who are the

The Doctrine of Ineffability

'happy owners of unspoilt perceptions', those who have 'vanquished the crystallizing tendencies of thought and attained an immediate if imperfect communion with reality'.[19]

It is readily seen how a doctrine which dismisses the ability of rational thoughts (presumably in the sense of *pure reason*) to touch reality, can easily degenerate still further into the position that rational expression of mystical reality is impossible; and the theological climate of today is such that apologists do not conclude that there may not be any God from the impossibility of evidential or rational confirmation, but that logic or rational language is an inadequate tool for grasping divine reality.

The third probable source of this notion stems from the close affinity between mysticism and mystery. There is first of all a strong etymological connection between the terms *mysticism* and *the mysteries*; according to Fleming, Ple and Boyer they spring from the same root. 'The word μυστικός comes from the verb μύω, which means "to close", and more particularly, to close the eyes. The earliest use we find of it in pre-Christian times is in connection with the Mystery religions, that is, with those cults whose essential rites were kept hidden from all but the initiated.'[20] And Fleming states, 'A mystic (μύστης), (in St. Paul's era when mystery cults flourished) was one initiated into Divine things: he must keep his mouth shut (μύειν) about them, because the initiation was secret.'[21] In this age the mystic was one initiated into the Eleusinian, Bacchic or Mithraic mysteries, not in the sense that he was introduced to private religious knowledge, but that he was conducted through a secret sacramental ritual. It was the details of this ritual which could not be disclosed to the uninitiated.

Bouyer has argued quite persuasively that although a line of historians from Harnack to Pére Festugiere have assumed that Christian mysticism has been infused with this Hellenistic sense of mystery, this could not be the case because the subject of Christian mystery is knowledge not ritual—a portion of reality inaccessible to reason or the senses. Hellenistic mystery was not expressed because it was legislatively forbidden for the religious ritual to be disclosed; Christian mystery was inexpressible because of its ineffable nature, that is, because it would not be verbally expressed.[22] However, Bouyer does not deny the connection between Christian mystery and mysticism—the fact that the element of mystery (in the Christian sense) within mysticism has resulted in a doctrine of the inexpressibility of mystical reality.

Having outlined this position and its probable origins let us now pay some critical attention to it.

If we say the statements of theology are significantly unlike other statements in that they are rationally attempting to express what is, by its metaphysical nature, inexpressible, we have established the uniqueness of divine commands; we have established that *nonsensical* statements such as *God wills X* are exempt from criticism directed toward meaningful utterances. In general this position has the merit of removing the sting of positivist sneers that theological statements are nonsense by thoroughly agreeing with this claim. The atheist and the theist here join hands. However, it offers a live alternative to the conclusion that religious matters can therefore be categorically dismissed by asserting the reality of the reference of nonsensical theological propositions.

Let me first make a few general remarks. To begin with, this position sacrifices too much for the sake of immunity from present-day criticism. It retreats into an impenetrable thicket of mystery gaining ontological assurance solely from God's private revelation. And this divine disclosure is by its nature incommunicable and unconfirmable. Russell's remarks are relevant here, that 'insight untested and unsupported, is an insufficient guarantee of truth, in spite of the fact that much of the most important truth is first suggested by its means. . . . Instinct, intuition or insight is what first leads to the beliefs which subsequent reason confirms or confutes.'[23] It is in fact quite impossible to differentiate illusion from inspiration at the pre-linguistic level. And as we said about Kierkegaard, if this position is not self-defeating, we are at least forced to rely entirely upon unreliable means for our knowledge of divine reality, without the benefit of public experience and disputation to question its authenticity.

And the *way of silence* cannot remain a category within the ranks of theology, although it may claim space as a religious category in a sociological classification, for silence is compatible with everything. This attempted inclusion is reminiscent of Inge's normative re-definition of *reason* for similar purposes of making mysticism more respectable. Witness the following extract: 'The mystic, then, is not, as such, a visionary: nor has he any interest in appealing to a faculty *above reason*, if reason is used in its proper sense as the logic of the whole personality.'[24] (It is curious, further, that *reason* here is for Inge what *myth* is for Reardon.)[25]

When we realize that a self-imposed silence not only sacrifices epistemological strength, but also inclusion in the market-place of theological claims, it is further apparent that assertion and denial are also logically forbidden to those advocating an inexpressibility doctrine. The retreat into silence cannot be broken for discursive reasoning concerning the reality or nature of the object of silent contemplation. I might add as a psychological adjunct, that the natural, exploratory instincts of the human imagination would demand answers to 'peripheral' religious questions which revelation failed to provide, thus driving those concerned with religion into theological discussion.

Another objection is this: It is highly doubtful whether there are any ineffable revealed truths. I say this neither because an allegedly inexpressible truth cannot be validated (although it seems to me that this position is somewhat persuasive), nor because of metaphysical presuppositions concerning the relationship between language and object, but simply because the revelations received by mystics are never new truths but beliefs which were previously known and derived from ordinary, highly verbalized sources. Pratt says, for example, that the communicated truths of the mystics 'are always old truths which they knew (though in a much less living form) before'[26]. 'Possibly *all* the mystical *revelations* may be accounted for as being first carried into the ecstasy by the mystic, and derived originally from social education, and all except this sense of presence may possibly be mere conclusions which the mystic comes to after reflecting upon his experience by a process of ordinary discursive thought; a number of mystics will be found to admit this. . . .'[27] Pratt states elsewhere that the 'mass of theological material which fills (the mystic's) mind' determines the content of mystical vision, and he cites Coe as saying that the mystic 'brings his theological beliefs to the mystical experience; he does not derive them from it'.[28] Just one of many examples illustrating the truth of this point is that Santa Teresa and Saint Ignatius Loyola mystically perceived the deep mystery of the holy Trinity only after reflecting upon this notion. I believe we have at work here a psychological device of self-assurance closely akin to that which enables the Catholic mystic to receive visions of Mary meditating rather than of Shiva dancing.

In general we can conclude that if the content of the mystic's revelation is a *truth* which has been stated elsewhere, his vision can hardly be called either original or, what is important to us, unutterable.

A further point is this: when a mystic claims that an experience cannot be expressed, he may not be bearing witness to a profundity, beyond the domain of language, but pleading his own inability to communicate an unusually moving experience. It is perfectly credible that the nature of an object of experience could be exceedingly recondite so that a person such as Machiavelli would not possess the aesthetic nature needed to seize and communicate it, and an artist like Proust would describe even its inner character to perfection. Intensely emotional experiences are difficult to describe and to some inadequately articulate souls, prohibitively difficult.

In specific circumstances, such a view may even be an expression of exasperation at a tough-minded listener, which means that to this unsympathetic person or such insensitive people the mystical vision is incommunicable. Obviously in any of these forms this position is not a serious philosophical threat.

However the doctrine of ineffability may not mean either an inability to convey profound experience or the impossibility of a reality being expressed. It might well mean that a believer is unwilling to reduce the holy, uncanny or mysterious to a

The Doctrine of Ineffability

linguistic level, feeling that to place it beside other describable objects defiles it and robs it of holy feeling. It is a recurrent view that the mere naming of a divine object renders it too manageable, too easily classified and reducible to inappropriate, familiar categories. Hence the Hebrew notion that God must not be named except on infrequent awesome occasions.

However, we cannot claim that we have knowledge of an experience (or an object), that is we cannot be consciously aware of having undergone a certain emotional experience, unless we have verbalized it. For the experience itself would remain an undifferentiated series of sensations unless it were separated and plucked from this opaque stream by a linguistic designation. It is in a class of states of feeling which cannot be truly known unless they are verbally symbolized. The statement, 'I am despondent' functions not only to describe one's feelings to others but enables the individual to become aware of his own feeling-state.

Finally, I might offer the linguistic criticism that there cannot logically be an *unutterable* because one item of knowledge which can be uttered about it is that it is unutterable. Paradoxically, the name itself provides a descriptive fact which necessarily allows of linguistic expression. And it does not help to label an ineffable reality by another name such as the *Divine Dark*, for once this *reality* is expressly characterized as unutterable it is thereby given the characteristic which can be uttered of it. Thus whether *unutterable* functions primarily as a noun standing for an ultimate reality, or solely as an adjective describing this reality called by another name, it is analytically self-defeating. It is actually in the same logical purlieu as that sister-term in negative theology *unknowable*, of which at least we know that it cannot be known. However, there are two important differences: In the first place the criticism against the unknowable can be rebutted by reference to the distinction between *knowledge of* and *knowledge about*. If *unknowable* is defined in terms of the former, then the characteristic of unknowability can conveniently be relegated to the latter category. Secondly, whereas an object or experience described as unutterable serves to delineate the area in which it can be sought, i.e. the pre-linguistic level, the ascription of unknowability logically compels us to terminate our search.

B: RUDOLF OTTO'S 'NUMINOUS'

Rudolf Otto's position seems to be a stronger one in that it stresses the non-rational element at the *heart* of religion. He claims that the experience of the *numinous*, a *mysterium tremendum*, awe-inspiring, holy and sacred at the core of religion, eludes conceptualization, hence the attempt to place it in propositional form necessarily results in nonsense. Otto does not want to say that religion in a broad sense cannot be conceptualized at all, as evidenced by remarks such as 'in religion there *is* very much that *can* be taught that is handed down in concepts and passed on in school instruction'.[29] And theological explanation is an admissible rational and linguistic procedure, otherwise Otto's efforts would be pointless. His book actually attempts a further analysis of that portion of religious feeling able to be expressed in concepts and that more essential part which is not—'this numinous basis and background to religion, which can only be induced, incited, and aroused.'[30]

Whether God's commands are exempt from the criticisms applicable to human commands depends in part upon the class of statements which remain utterable after statements purporting to refer to the experience of the numinous have been discarded. If *is* statements expressing God's will are grouped with expressions of the numinous, then we avoid certain moral judgments being applicable to them at the expense of affirming the impossibility of conceptualizing God's commands. And since the derivation of *X is good* depends upon the possibility of translating the experience of God's commands into a meaningful verbal concept, we are also precluded from legitimately deriving this evaluative proposition. (We may derive a meaningful conclusion when the premises of a syllogism are irredeemable nonsense, just as a true conclusion can be derived from false premises; however, this is a freak occurrence allowed by the formal scheme of logic.) If, on the other hand, God's will is not inexpressible then like Fitzgerald's

The Doctrine of Ineffability

'Omar', we 'Came out by the same door wherein [we] went'. It is incumbent upon us to show in what logically significant way propositions expressing God's will differ from propositions expressing man's will.

Actually, when we attempt to analyse Otto's coinage rigorously, when we attempt to chart the limits of the *unutterable* to ascertain whether expressions of God's commands fall within the boundary, we reach some curious conclusions. We find that according to the remarks which Otto makes specifically on the means of expression of the numinous, nothing is truly unutterable! We find that the line of demarcation does not fall between the expressible and the inexpressible as Otto's earlier remarks might lead one to believe, but between the expressible which can be publicly understood and the expressible which possesses an exclusively esoteric meaningfulness. The latter category contains utterances (as well as reverent gestures, attitudes, etc.) which can only be received and understood by those with 'an inborn capacity to receive and understand', he who has 'the spirit in the heart'; 'where the wind of the spirit blows, there the mere *rational* terms themselves are imbued with power to arouse the feeling of the "non-rational"'.... 'He who in the spirit reads the written word lives in the numinous.' In other words, one way of receiving knowledge of the non-rational numinous is *via* the rational expression correctly approached; another method of gaining knowledge of this same numinous is by a direct non-rational apprehension. (Otto often uses *non-rational* to stand for both an epistemological channel and a metaphysical category which makes interpretation difficult.) Otto's views then resolve into a Protestantism reminiscent of Schleiermacher's position that theological expressions refer to the inner experiences of a select few and must be *decoded* to gain universal meaning, or somewhat similar to Barth's beliefs that a special miracle of grace is needed to render Biblical assertions meaningful.

However, before we conclude from this that *God wills X* can be meaningfully articulated either as an utterance which has meaning for the initiated, or one which makes sense on an ordinary level, it is well to point out that an *utterance* and a *concept* are not synonymous. Although Otto often uses them interchangeably so that one might be led to equate them (as McPherson does in *New Essays in Philosophical Theology*), not everything which can be rationally uttered can be conceptualized. The numinous experience, in fact, cannot be packed into concepts although it can be expressed in esoterically meaningful words. Thus our question actually reduces to the following: Are utterances of the sort *God wills X*, that is, divine commands, utterances which have public or private meaning, or an attempt to conceptualize that which is incapable of being conceptualized? (Short of making this distinction I cannot see any way of saving Otto from a charge of grossly inconsistent and muddled thinking.) The answer to this question surely must be that it can be either, depending upon what is substituted for X.

If God is said to command things such as 'make haste' (2 Chron. xxxv. 21), 'Stretch out thine hand' (Exod. x. 12), 'sit down' (Mark vi. 39), or 'Come thou and all thy house into the ark' (Gen. vii. 1), then we can hardly call these expressions of concepts. However, if we take the following examples, 'Honour thy father and thy mother' (Mat. xv. 4), 'Thou shalt not kill' (Exod. xx. 13), 'love one another, as I have loved you' (John xv. 12), or 'Thou shalt have no other gods before me' (Exod. xx. 3), in this sense, commandments are concepts. And without engaging in detailed classification of all divine commands, I believe it will be allowed that we are exclusively concerned with the latter class of utterances, the latter meaning of divine imperative in our present inquiry. That is to say, the type of command issued by deity that exhorts or demands obedience to a principle, rather than satisfaction of a particular wish.

Having analysed Otto's position in this way we can conclude that God's commands, as concepts, are ineffable. This aspect of Otto's ideas is surely untenable for several of the reasons (*mutatis mutandis*) outlined in the previous section. And as for that portion of Otto's position which resembles Schleiermacher's thought in affirming the private nature of a considerable portion of religious discourse, let me put forward the following objection—an objection contained in Wittgenstein's *Philosophical Investigations*.

The Doctrine of Ineffability

The point is simply that logically speaking there cannot be a private language referring to unique inner experience any more than there can be utterances so logically idiosyncratic that they are *eo ipso* precluded from becoming meaningful outside an esoteric realm of discourse. For language, insofar as it functions to identify, transmit, name, etc., experience, by its very nature is not a private thing no matter how private the experience to which it refers. In fact, one learns how to use language by learning the essentially public rules governing the use of words. Then we find the application of these words in our private experience rather than first inventing words to describe personal happenings. Wittgenstein uses the example of *pain* and *sensation* to point out the fact that even these terms referring to intensely private experience are words which are taught and learned publicly. 'Now, what about the language which describes my inner experiences and which only I myself can understand? *How* do I use words to stand for my sensations?—As we ordinarily do? Then are my words for sensations tied up with my natural expressions of sensation? In that case my language is not a private one.'[31]

It follows, therefore, that if those professing that theological utterances gain their meaningfulness by referring to the unique inner experience of a fortunate few, or can only be rendered meaningful by a special miracle of grace, are simply failing to recognize that language, even religious language, is not a private code but is essentially public in nature. It does not require decoding as do perhaps *Ball shoe elephant stamp* or *Gyre and gimble in the wabe*; it is not so nonsensical that our only recourse in rendering it meaningful is to claim that it refers to special inner experience. Religious language exhibits numerous major features in common with ordinary linguistic expressions. MacIntyre once quoted Sir Edwyn Hoskyn's remark that since the language of the Bible is a familiar one, a special miracle of grace may be required to render Biblical assertions important, but it is not necessary to finding them meaningful.

I believe we can conclude that when theologians speak of religious utterances becoming *more deeply meaningful* or gaining

Deity and Morality

meaning on a *more fundamental level* that they are actually speaking of the way in which an expression could be *acceptable* or *significant*. Also, that when a position is advanced which pivots around the notion of esoterically meaningful language, that it can be rebutted on logical grounds.

NOTES

Chapter V

1. Butler, Dom. C., *Western Mysticism*, London, Constable and Co., Ltd, 1927, p. 188.
2. Knowles, D., *The English Mystical Tradition*, London, Burns and Oates, 1961, p. 3.
3. James, W., *The Varieties of Religious Experience*, New York, Longmans, Green and Co., 1923, p. 380.
4. *The Works of Tennyson*, ed. by Hallam Lord Tennyson, London, Macmillan & Co., 1913, p. 551.
5. Stutfield, H. E. M., *Mysticism and Catholicism*, London, J. Fisher Unwin Ltd., 1925, pp. 31–33. Cf. also Maeterlinck, M., *Le Grand Secret*, Paris, E. Frasquelle, 1921, pp. 192–213.
6. Underhill, E., *Mysticism*, London, Methuen and Co. Ltd., 1916, Part I, Ch. VI, pp. 149–77.
7. Récéjac, J. E., *Essai Sur Les Fondements de la Connaissance Mystique*, Paris, F. Alcan, 1897, Part II, pp. 85–181.
8. Gregory, E. C., *An Introduction to Christian Mysticism*, London, Allenson, 1908, Part II.
9. Nettleship, R. L., *Philosophical Remains*, ed. by A. C. Bradley, London, Oxford University Press, 1901, pp. 25–32.
10. Macintyre, A., 'The Logical Status of Religious Belief', in *Metaphysical Beliefs*, ed. by A. Macintyre, London, S. C. M. Press Ltd, 1957, p. 178.
11. Inge expresses a similar analysis of mystical expressions as poetic symbols; however, he further holds that these symbols soon lose their religious content and repudiate their mystical origin by becoming petrified or evaporated. Inge, W. R., *Christian Mysticism*, London, Methuen and Co., Ltd., 1933, p. 5.
12. Cf. Suzuki, D. J., *An Introduction to Zen Buddhism*, New York, The Philosophical Library, 1949.
13. Peers, E. A., *Studies of the Spanish Mystics*, London, Sheldon Press, 1927, pp. 376–8.
14. Hocking, W. E., *The Meaning of God in Human Experience*, New Haven, Yale University Press, 1924, 6th Edition, pp. 37–8, Ch. V *passim*.

15. Underhill, E., *The Mystic Way*, London, J. M. Dent & Sons Ltd., 1913, *passim*.
16. Pratt, J. B., *Psychology of Religious Belief*, London, Macmillan & Co., 1907, p. 302, Ch. X *passim*.
17. Cordelier, J., *The Spiral Way*, London, John M. Watkins, 1922, pp. 56-69.
18. Underhill, E., *ibid.*, p. 8.
19. Underhill, E., loc. cit.
20. Bouyer, L., 'Mysticism, An Essay on the History of a Word', in *Mystery and Mysticism*, London, Blackfriars, 1956, pp. 121-3.
21. Fleming, W. K., *Mysticism in Christianity*, London, Robert Scott, 1933, pp. 8-9.
22. Cf. Thornton, L. S., 'The Christian Conception of God,' in *Essays Catholic and Critical*, ed. by E. G. Selwyn, New York, Macmillan Co., 1950, pp. 130-4.
23. Russell, B., 'Mysticism and Logic', *Hibbert Journal*, Vol. XII, No. 4, July 1914.
24. Inge, W. R., *Christian Mysticism*, p. 19.
25. Cf. Reardon, B. M. G., 'Philosophy and Myth', *Theology*, Vol. LXV, No. 502, April 1962.
26. Pratt, J. B., *The Religious Consciousness*, New York, Macmillan and Co., 1940, p. 410.
27. Pratt, J. B., *ibid.*, p. 412.
28. *Ibid.*, p. 450. Cf. also Leuba, J. H., *The Psychology of Religious Mysticism*, New York, Harcourt, Brace and Co., 1925.
29. Otto, R., *The Idea of the Holy*, trans. by J. W. Harvey, London, Oxford Univ. Press, 1923, p. 62.
30. *Ibid.*, p. 63.
31. Wittgenstein, L., *Philosophical Investigations*, trans. by G. E. M. Anscombe, Oxford, Basil Blackwell, 1958, p. 91e, (256).

Chapter VI

RELIGIOUS DISCOURSE AND POETIC LANGUAGE

A: REVELATION AND INSPIRATION

We have already seen (Chapter V, Part A) that those verbose mystics who, in apparent self-contradiction ascribe ineffability to their visions, actually mean that mystical reality cannot be expressed except in poetic images or symbols. In order to supply an account of divine reality, appropriate images must be evoked by means of poetic expressions. The revelation received by these mystics is not incommunicable but it is not amenable to expression in ordinary terms either; poetic language must be employed which strains the limits of linguistic meaning almost to the point of rupture to convey a reality almost beyond expression. Just as French and Spanish possess various refinements of tense which the English language does not contain and moods which it cannot convey, so the language of poetry is able to communicate certain forms or aspects of existence which cannot be crystallized in the pedantic, niggling language of proposition. If Hegel is correct in placing religion between art and philosophy in his system, we can understand even more clearly how when rational expression of divine truth is discredited, poetic language may be elevated.

This is, in fact, another mode of characterizing religious utterances—in terms of poetic images, metaphor symbols, etc. And it is quite natural to do so as a pleasant alternative to a doctrine of ineffability. To some extent drawing parallels between religious language and poetic language has also been an emergency door for desperate theologians who have witnessed the corpus of theology threatened by assaults on the epistemological basis of belief, the logical structure of apologetic argument, and the ultimate authority of Scripture. When pressed for a definitive and valid account of the logical nature of religious language, or when such an account cannot be cogently presented and theological language is taken to be meaningless, it is an enormous temptation to explain one logically obscure stratum of discourse in terms of another, particularly when the latter, poetic language, has a respectable standing.

Comparisons of religious discourse with strata of language acknowledged to be largely exempt from rigorous logical scrutiny are particularly welcome to the harassed believer who has progressively witnessed Bibliolatry ridiculed, the mechanical inspiration of Biblical writing rejected, and the infallibility of Scriptural authority abandoned under the attack of textual critics. To such individuals still bewildered even by the enlightenment criticism of Haeckel and Voltaire, it must be a profound relief to interpret the extraordinary language powers of Balaam's ass and the arrested motion of Joshua's sun as poetic images. However, we must set cynicism aside and admit that the analogy was not stumbled upon as a desperate expedient any more than as an alternative to an ineffability doctrine. It arose primarily out of a perception of the obvious way in which poetry and religion are bed-fellows.

In a broad sense all of the sensuous elements of worship point up the close affinities which exist between poetry and religion. Such items as organ music, incense, chants, candles, hymns, ceremonial robes, symbols, icons and the cathedral architecture itself unite in making an almost irresistible aesthetic appeal to our senses. Furthermore (and more importantly for our purposes), one has only to cast a cursory glance at the language of Scripture to realize that the commands, historical accounts, psalms, prayers, prophecy, moral injunctions, etc., are presented in an aesthetically ornate, evocative style. The linguistic texture of the Bible, its assonance, metaphor, rhyme, grandiloquent tone and sublime subject satisfy the essential requirements for poetry. The King James Bible in particular could be favourably compared for artistic merit with the best of Milton and Dante. (A similar claim might well be made for the Bhagavadgita and the Koran as well.)

Deity and Morality

We might also add as a corrollary that religious expression like poetic expression cannot be understood on a strictly literal level. Neither one is a set of propositions exclusively capable of rational comprehension or handling, but employs language rich in associations beyond themselves. Therefore we must judge both types of discourse in similar logical terms.

And before taking leave of this point we might also mention that illuminating parallels can be witnessed in such linguistic aspects of both religion and poetry as emotive power, aesthetic appeal, internal inconsistencies[1] (which somehow do not damage the force of the message), solemn tone, a certain emotional enchantment (which Plato denounced as inducing uncritical acceptance), momentous subject-matter, unconfirmability, etc. All of these items persuade the theologian to affirm significant parallels, if not a logical identity, between the structure of poetic language and the structure of religious language.

Now by placing theological assertions in the category of purely poetic expressions, we certainly render the assertion *God wills X* exempt from moral judgment. Clearly to say that we must judge everything that God wills to be good before obeying it, or in general to invoke the naturalistic fallacy, is totally inappropriate when as an utterance without cognitive meaning expressions of God's will function to evoke rather than inform. We are here flogging a dead horse. However, by the same token we cannot reach the moral conclusion that *X is good* when the proposition *God wills X* has merely poetic meaning, unless we are prepared to say that this is an emotional response. We may question the impossibility of deriving evaluative conclusions from descriptive premises but we cannot claim that a moral conclusion can be derived from premises which have purely evocative meaning (unless, perhaps, we maintain an emotive theory of ethics which is repugnant to the theologian).

Furthermore, it is fatal to give theological assertions the status of simple poetic expressions because this would make all of theology an intricate system of evocative utterances. This is not only a peculiarly difficult view to maintain, but it hardly serves as an adequate characterization of religion, to empty such central notions and revelation of cognitive content. Theologians would leap to assert claims of factual truth to theological propositions; they would maintain that theological statements have an actual reference and that theological propositions are pre-eminently informative. In the proposition under discussion, the theologian would not be content with the interpretation of *God wills X* as an emotive utterance designed, for example, to induce a feeling of security but would claim that a state of affairs is being asserted. And this insistence upon cognitive meaning, upon denotation as well as connotation, throws us back into our difficulties in significantly differentiating *God wills X* from *the premier wills X*. The examination of the accounts of the logical status of theological discourse was begun, it will be remembered, in the hope of exposing a radical difference of such a nature as to render certain criticism irrelevant or pointless.

This view that religion is *mere* poetry, i.e. only an integrated complex of emotive expressions is, in fact, almost exclusively maintained by unbelievers who are quite convinced that the claims of religion are groundless. Such critics cannot deny that religious experience and language do evoke basic emotions in human beings and has other affinities with poetry. However, having allowed this much, they will not admit that any truth-claims can be inferred. They quite validly hold that *demands of emotion* do not entail metaphysical conclusions any more than *demands of reason* do, although both sorts of *demands* can lead us to understand why, for example, monistic or theistic notions are held. However, rather than throwing out the baby with the bath water (or *vice versa*), they desire to retain the poetic form of religious expression for its aesthetic merits.[2]

It has been argued, of course, that the poetic imagination itself, or the evocative texture of poetry, is fundamentally intertwined with truth; that the philosophical distinction revered from Plato to Baumgarten between *Truth* and *Beauty* is a false dichotomy. Since poetry grasps and embodies truth, the question of the truth-value of creative, poetic expressions does not arise. This point is usually pressed by affirming the *identity* of imagination or inspiration with revelation. An inspired poet, it is maintained, is one in receipt of divine revelation, his imaginative insight guaranteeing the truth of his *nisus formativus*. Murry, for example, says that great poetry 'is the direct embodiment through symbols which are necessarily dark, of a pure comprehensive and self-satisfying experience, which we may call, if we please, an immediate intuition into the hidden nature of things'. For Murry, as for H. D. Lewis, 'art is itself a divine revelation'.[3]

In these circumstances, in which art is regarded as a mode of religious awareness, it is perfectly legitimate to sanctify imaginative art as apprehended truth; poetry can safely be treated as authoritative doctrine because the poet is in Farrer's sense a prophet. If this view is taken then demythologizing or the depoeticizing of Scripture is an impossible task, for to discard this aesthetic element of the Bible is to throw out inspirational truth as well. This entire position is buttressed by common acknowledgements that the poet, through his heightened imagination and sensitivity does perceive certain visions beyond the reach of the apologist. We have returned to Underhill's point that the artist and poet are the 'happy owners of unspoilt perceptions' who have attained communion with reality. In every religion it does seem that the insights of a gifted spiritual leader furnish the stuff out of which dogma develops. H. D. Lewis says at one point that 'the artist is, in the first instance, a seer, and his essential function, in his relation to others, is to make them see something to which they are normally blind. This may be something in nature or in human life; it does not matter which. But we must in some way be made aware of objects and events in a fashion which is like seeing them for the first time. The artist wrests their secrets from objects and makes them glow with a distinctiveness which escapes normal consciousness of them. This illumination of the world which almost amounts to a transformation is the essential feature of art . . .'[4]

This sharp affinity which is felt between religious and poetic insight, or artistic inspiration and religious revelation, has a distinguished history. It originated in the Greek conception of a poet as, quite literally, a direct recipient of divine messages.

Religious Discourse and Poetic Language

Poets were regarded as divinely inspired oracles or seers in possession of infallible truths and as such occupied a high position in Greek society and culture. Homer, for example, was not only valued as a gifted poet but *eo ipso*, an inspired religious teacher—even the fount of all knowledge.

Numerous writers have maintained that it was because of this distasteful, unwarranted reverence for poets that Plato launched his attack upon poetry and denied poets inclusion in his ideal state. His tirade against Homer in Book II, 379 C, ff, and Book III, 386 A, ff. of the *Republic*, in which he criticizes passages from the poet which have a corrupting influence rather than being beneficial or true, is often cited in evidence. Other commentators such as George Ainslie Hight and Professor Wilamowitz-Mollendorf using similar passages (e.g. *Republic*, Book X, 595A, 603A–608A; *Gorgias*, 501E–502E; *Laws*, Book III, 682A, 700–701, etc.) conclude that Plato did not categorically denounce poetry but only that poetry which tended to incite undesirable emotions. This view has the outstanding merit of resolving the inconsistency between Plato's denunciation of poetry and the deliberate poetic style of the Dialogues. In any case, Plato certainly opposed the conception of poetry in an Athens which sanctified the *Iliad* and the *Odyssey*, and he would be unwilling to identify Homer or any other poet as a philospher-king or seer.

However, the decisive objection which I see to identifying great poetry with profound truth is simply that the logically absurd situation would arise where mutually contradictory notions would have an equal truth-claim provided they were expressed by a gifted poet. The imaginative fables of the Homeric Hymns would stand on equal footing with the Gospel of St Mark. It must be concluded that since this criterion for truth commits us to asserting the validity of incompatible notions, what is beautiful cannot be the measure of what is true. An act of rational discernment or judgement is essential to differentiate between what is aesthetically moving and the sensuously expressed profundity, the appeals made to our senses alone from those which offer truth insights. Santayana once said in correcting the erroneous impression that Browning's poetry presented a coherent, rational meaning of life, that 'Awakening may be mistaken for enlightenment, and the galvanizing of torpid sensations and impulses for wisdom'.[5]

Another major objection is this: if the inspirational sources of great poetry and religious truth are identical, how is secular poetry to be accounted for? To say it is not *genuine* poetry will not be satisfactory if for no other reason than that Shakespeare, surely one of the greatest poets, was not a religious writer. It is equally insufficient to regard secular poetry as latently religious because critics are in unanimous agreement that in the works of numerous poets including Shakespeare, there is neither an explicit nor an implicit religious element. (Shakespeare, in fact, did not have a particular point of view in his sonnets or plays.) And what is one to do with the Greek poets who were religiously oriented but hardly in the Judaeo-Christian tradition. If *inspired* as a quasi-descriptive, quasi-commendatory term, is to be employed generically to include Christian and pagan poets such as Dante and Homer, then we cannot identify Christian revelation and poetic inspiration. And if it is applied to religious and secular poets such as Milton and Shakespeare, then religious revelation and poetic inspiration cannot be equated.

However, I do not believe that Austin Farrer succeeds in separating inspiration and revelation by saying that the poet and prophet share the 'technique of inspiration', that 'both move an incantation of images under a control', but, 'The controls are not the same, and therefore the whole nature and purpose of the two utterances go widely apart: the poet is a maker, the prophet is a mouthpiece'.[6] Unless Farrer is willing to support a mechanical view of inspiration, he must allow for the moulding and shaping influence of the individual prophet's poetic genius, however much they 'had their minds charged with the word of God'. Actually, I cannot believe that Farrer supports a statement such as this: 'his [the prophet's] control tells him exactly what to say, for he is not responding to the quality of human life, he is responding to the demands of eternal will on Israel . . .',[7] for this statement tends to contradict numerous previous ones. And the poet surely is not only a *maker* in the sense of an imaginative creator or manufacturer of images or notions, but in some sense the inspired bearer of profound truth as well.

I would also reject Farrer's second distinction which he outlines as follows: 'The poem expresses whatever of the infinite aspects of human existence it does express: what it does not express, it leaves unexpressed. One can never say *The poet ought to have been saying so and so, but he has only succeeded in saying this*. There is nothing that he ought to have been saying except what he has said. All life is open to him: let him say what the Muse prompts him to say. He may not say much, or he may not say it well, but he cannot say the wrong thing.'[8]

I should have thought that both the content of poetry and the content of prophecy, that is the particular ideas expressed, can both admit of rightness and wrongness by reference to determinate criterion, i.e. an evaluative, theological, or metaphysical system. Milton might well be judged wrong in saying: 'They also serve who only stand and wait' just as the author of Exodus could be regarded as wrong in saying 'Life for life, Eye for eye, Tooth for tooth, Hand for hand', etc. And if we interpret *wrong* as contrary to fact, which is closer to Farrer's meaning here, there are numerous cases of erroneous statements of scientific facts which are to be found in ancient poetry and ancient Scripture alike. Surely here we can judge the utterances of the poet as well as the prophet wrong in a perfectly straightforward way. And it is equally appropriate to say that particular poets or prophets have not said much, or on aesthetic grounds, that they have expressed their thoughts quite badly.

In the following paragraph of his book, Farrer goes a bit further and declares that what the prophet 'has got to say is determinate and particular, it is what the Lord God declares and requires on the day on which he speaks'.[9] If this is the acid test or touchstone for that which a writer is right in saying (and it must be observed that this is an astonishingly harsh interpretation of revelation), then the promptings of the Muse on a particular day would furnish equal proof against error. We cannot argue from the fact that a message was inspired either that it was intended to be communicated on a particular day or that God rather than the

Muse inspired it. I might add that Farrer's earlier attempts to declare certain images 'revealed images' since they are 'authoritatively communicated',[10] collapses by virtue of similar unsupported suppositions.

We could carry the discussion concerning inspiration and revelation further, and summon strident philosophical voices declaring either the identity or dissimilarity between poetry and prophecy. However, having demonstrated the untenability of the argument which attempts to legitimate the poetic conception of religious language by saying that in this way truth is automatically conveyed, I believe it is pointless to press the positive side of the controversy any further.

Before taking leave of this entire topic, however, another essential point must be made.

This point has been somewhat repressed to give full play to the notion of religious utterances as purely emotive, poetic expressions. We have been speaking as if an interpretation of religious language as logically akin to poetic language means a reduction to a purely emotive level of meaning. On this reading I hope I have shown that the position is untenable. However, it is illegitimate to equate *poetic* with *emotive* or *evocative* without remainder because poetic language always contains a cognitive element. Language, in fact, cannot evoke emotion without being somewhat informative. In this it is unlike music which makes its affective appeal directly through the senses. It is a medium which, by its nature, must possess and convey material for the understanding. This is abundantly clear in the works of Byron, Shelley and Keats, but it can even be seen in poetry which hovers on the fringe of painting and music. As an example of this I would cite James Joyce whose liquid, musical language in *Ulysses* and *Finnegan's Wake* seems to envelop the reader as a symphony would. In *Ulysses* we read passages in which language is terribly strained and tortured: 'Woodshadows floated silently by through the morning peace from the stairhead seaward where he gazed. Inshore and farther out the mirror of water whitened, spurned by lightshod hurrying feet.'[11] And in *Finnegan's Wake* we discover perhaps the farthest boundaries of language: 'There's

where. First. We pass through grass behush the bush to. Whisk!
A gull. Gulls. Far calls. Coming, far! End here. Us then. Finn,
again! Take. Bussoftlhee, mememormee! Till thousendsthee.
Lps. The key to. Given! A way a lone a last a loved a
long the.'[12]

It is quite true that we are charmed by the musical cadence of these lines, the sonorous vocabulary and waving rhythm of the prose, and that the language seems to tumble and swirl like music, however, we would not receive even undifferentiated sensations unless some cognitive impressions were conveyed. It is truly fragmented and distorted like a dream yet the words themselves are not meaningless but on the contrary contain compressed meanings which expand to a wide range of references and connotations. A phrase like "wavewhitewedded words' may be difficult to understand, perhaps even nonsensical as a composite whole, yet it creates an impression (a visual image) because of our understanding of the meaning of the individual terms. Without this we would have neither language nor words but a collection of letters or phonetic sounds. Without begging the question by building arbitrary and desirable characteristics into the term *language*, I believe we can conclude that language cannot be evocative without being informative.

If this position is a valid one, then religious discourse and even theological statements can be regarded as logically parallel to poetic language without fear of automatically extracting all cognitive content (and all truth claims). And for reasons mentioned earlier, the parallel can be considerably illuminating to religious discourse. However, without tracing every thread of logical similarity which is of support or succour to the theologian, we can see that the principal problem which this approach faces is that of differentiating the cognitive from the emotive elements. It transforms our basic problem into a consideration of whether God's commands, as poetic expressions, possess *sufficient* informativeness to be liable to cognitive criticism.

I would answer this in the same way that a similar problem was handled in the section on Rudolf Otto (Chapter V, Part B), concerning whether divine commands constituted concepts.

Deity and Morality

God's commands can either be principally emotive or informative depending upon the particular expression of the command. However, it is beyond all genuinely valid objections or cavil to say that the preponderate group would contain commands which were either principally informative or sufficiently informative to qualify for cognitive scrutiny.

Once we have granted this, the concept of poetry is no longer an impregnable citadel within which religious language can gain asylum. For on these terms religious language is not placed in a sufficiently unique position to render it immune from the type of cognitive criticism which moral philosophers, for example, bring to bear. On this reading it is still perfectly relevant to ask if that which God commands is in fact good.

In general, however, the logical comparison between poetic discourses and religious discourse seems both illuminating and valid.

B: MYTHS AND IMAGES

A position closely connected with the one described above does not award centrality to poetry in general but to the conception of myth. The word *myth* is understood in common speech as an imaginative story or fable, that is, as a fictitious but entertaining product of uncritical, primitive peoples. Even more sophisticated judgements have often held that myths make fascinating study for the anthropologist or sociologist concerned with primitive religion, but scarcely deserves inclusion among the verifiable propositions of science. However, in the nineteenth century, interest was revived among both secular scholars and theologians in the notion that myths are an original and necessary means of metaphysical expression, that mythological themes express elements of religious awareness inexpressible in any other form. (On this reading it is as exclusive as similar conceptions of religious expression in poetic terms.) Berdyaev describes myth as 'the concrete recital of events and original phenomena of the spiritual life symbolized in the natural world, which has engraved itself on the language, memory and creative energy of the people.'[13] This is the view which has recently gained considerable popularity.

Not only are *rational myths* such as Artemis of the *Odyssey* or the Homeric conception of Zeus regarding as revealing images, but even the irrational myths which Müller calls 'the silly, savage and senseless element' such as the metamorphoses of men or gods into animals, trees or stars.[14] Instead of attempting to separate unattractive or absurd myths from Christian narratives, by saying that the former are heavily disguised and distorted historical accounts of men as Enemerus and later Banier did,[15] or to say that myths were invented by legislators 'to persuade the many and to be used in support of law'[16] as Aristotle did, the modern movement insists that all myth is valuable in so far as it is the essential form in which man reconciles his relationship with nature and the universe. It is 'an organic function of the culture within which it occurs', 'an original and spontaneous form of human understanding, valuable precisely as such. . . . It secures a practical harmony between man himself and an environment otherwise impenetrably mysterious and menacing.'[17]

Schelling produced a seminal work in the nineteenth century[18] which gave great force to what may be called the myth movement in theology. In his book Schelling fully explored the conception of myth on the assumption that it was a necessary vehicle for expressing our most fundamental relationship with the universe. He maintained that through myths, nature, man and society were harmonized into an organic unity; that the animistic urges of human consciousness and basic primitive experiences universally common to man in his dealings with nature are here given adequate expression. Schelling's nineteenth-century Romanticism (culminating in a transcendental idealism in which nature and spirit were joined in a series of *developments*), regarded myth as 'a necessary moment in the process of self-unfolding or self-development of the Absolute'. All religious myths, even the crudest polytheism of nature religions were necessary stages to an apprehension of ethical monotheism.[19] Berdyaev also struck this note by emphasizing how the myths of the Fall and Prometheus symbolize central moral or spiritual events in man or in man's relationship with nature.[20] These 'basic life phenomena' are symbolized in a dynamic way, which is, perhaps, the only way of grasping them.

For every sympathetic writer on this subject, myth is at the very least valued for its psychological benefits. By irrationally stressing the harmony of identity between appearance and reality, rather than any essential dualism, it induces a feeling of knowledge and control over the universe. Everything is as it seems to be. In addition, the individual ceases to rely upon individual reason as the final determinant of truth in favour of the group beliefs. If one person perceives disharmony in the universe, for example, the force of the common mythological beliefs in its sympathy and unity aids in overcoming fears of threatening forces. Myth also provides reassurance by lifting supernatural events out of an eternal flux and positioning them in time and space. The reports of these specific occurrences within physical and temporal dimensions brings the supernatural into comfortable perspective. Like an icon or holy image, myth renders the eternal somewhat finite and tangible.[21]

Of course, in an attempt to sufficiently broaden the concept of myth, to lift it out of its resting-place beside fable, fairy tale and old wive's tale, and grant it a respectable status by virtue of its expression of basic human longings for integration with the universe, theologians are tending to inflate the notion out of all sensible proportions. The pendulum appears to have swung too far. Reardon, for example, argues that since myth's inherent purpose is the articulation of 'man's sense of his own existence', religion 'as a projection of the mythical consciousness', and philosophy as a 'myth passed through the solvent of reason', ... 'can claim to be necessary for the authentification of man's being'.[22] In order to stretch myth to cover philosophy Reardon equates it with metaphysical assumptions, such as those made by the logical positivists concerning the 'rational acceptability' of 'physicalism' and the 'unity of science' as well as various constructions of Kant and Hegel. To add further weight to his point, philosophy and myth are contrasted with science whose method is 'abstract and generalizing, its standpoint morally neutral';

'science, which tends always to eliminate the particular and temporary as irrelevant'.[24]

In the first place, myth is not just any metaphysical assumption but one of a particular kind. That is to say, although all myths may be metaphysical assumptions, not all metaphysical assumptions are myths. The metaphysics of mythology are usually *argumentum ad hominem*, particularly geared to psychological needs, and in that sense rationalizations *par excellence*, whereas those of philosophy (even the absurdities of some system-builders) are pre-eminently rational attempts to analyse, interpret and/or explain certain aspects of experience. Even if this is denied (and I fail to see how it can be), it must be admitted that philosophy is not only or mainly an enterprise devoted to constructing metaphysical theories. The writer of this article is sufficiently aware of contemporary philosophy to appreciate this. And to label rational assumptions concerning the regularity of nature, the revealing character of language or the value of logical analysis as myths, on all fours with such myth themes as those concerning childbirth, death, destiny, puberty and the hereafter is to violate the entire concept. It is only when myth and philosophy are defined in a strained and peculiar way that any similarity is possible between the two. In addition although myth and religion can be regarded as concentrating upon *the particular*, finding the time and place of '*this* man' and '*that* woman' significant as Reardon suggests, philosophy (outside of Existentialism) certainly bears a closer resemblance to science in its method of generalization and abstraction.[25] If the scientific method is taken as diametrically opposed to the myth-creating method (as it seems to be) then on this distinction alone our case is won.

A principal variation of the above theological approach is that of the *image-theologian* who attempts a Biblical exegesis in terms of certain key images. L. S. Thornton and Austin Farrer in particular have devoted several books[26] to examining the nature of the major symbols and images present in the Bible, as Creuzer did before them.[27] Numerous typologists and image-theologians like Farrer have been thrown up who regard Scripture as an intricate pattern of symbols and images, astonishingly interconnected and cohesive. The obvious, incidental metaphors, such as 'my rock and my fortress' are not referred to, but the overall configurative images such as the *Suffering Servant, Son of Man* and the *Throne of David*.[28] These larger, more persistent images are traced through the books of the Bible and are taken to be interpretative, archetypal images, revealing the relationship between humanity and deity. These images, which man has repeatedly returned to (or God has quite consistently revealed) are taken as symbols of an underlying, fundamental truth. It is assumed that 'Revelation recapitulates the same thematic material' in the religious history; that the unity or image-patterns which the typologist discovers is highly significant, especially in view of the vast historical and cultural differences which exist, for example, between the writings of Genesis and Revelation.

Several general criticisms of this position could be offered: One danger in accepting this approach is that recurrent symbols and myths might persuade us of the reality of unreal entities and the truth of false ideas. We cannot exclude this possibility by definition; the historical persistence of a religious myth or symbol is not an automatic guarantee of its fundamental metaphysical roots but only its satisfaction of timeless human cravings. The coherence and integrating power of Scriptural images or the basic myths of mankind may tell us something about human beings, however, it is an unwarranted assumption that ontological or metaphysical truth is being transmitted. Put differently, the psychologically beneficial myth, the organically developed or complex-patterned, tightly-integrated myth *tamen usque recurret* is not to be identified with the true, for these facts simply have not any apologetic implications. The systematic coherence theory of truth has been consistently attacked on this very point.[29]

I fail to see any validity in claims of this nature. To my mind the following kind of statement is typical of the muddled thinking which is employed in justification of this approach. 'Now the onus of proof lies on him who *denies* connection between the *structure* of our minds and the structure of reality—between our intellectual instincts and the data which our intellects study, for thought and reality are not separate entities separated by a gulf; subject and object are abstractions from a concrete whole. We have, therefore, every right to regard our intellectual *demand* for unity as far more than a demand—as being an insight.'[30] This illogical reasoning is often employed, *mutatis mutandis*, in establishing the connection between the unity or coherence of myths or images and reality. Tillich clearly recognized the absurdity of a 'flotilla of symbols . . . adrift, unpiloted' without one direct proposition to validate the oblique language. (For Tillich the one proposition being 'God is Being—itself.') This would surely provide an improved metaphysics for the image-theologian.

Another objection is this. What is there in the nature of the *persistence* of an image or myth which ought to induce our belief in its relationship with divine reality? Why should we accept and respect just those images which continually reappear? As H. D. Lewis points out in criticizing Jung's view that we have an innate tendency to form certain kinds of images in certain situations, 'dominant images, whether they arise from the course our experience takes or from some native propensity to form them, do not, by the mere fact of being dominant or being made inevitable for us in some fundamental way, acquire a religious character . . . there is nothing in the fact of being innate or very pervasive to establish a proper linkage of any of our images with . . . religious insights.'[31]

It seems to me quite plausible that a *unique* image could be the vehicle for divine revelation rather than recurrent ones. In fact, an argument grounded in the uniqueness of the message of Jesus (if not the image) has often been employed to prove its divine origins. I cannot see an overwhelming argument in favour of uniqueness or recurrence. However, if the option were forced I would elect the uniqueness approach, for the astonishing persistence of certain myths or images is more likely to have its origin in the strictly human situation, the common position of man in relation to the universe. And divine revelation is more likely to impinge upon the human consciousness, producing a unique departure from well-trodden thought grounded in human needs and desires. We have more probably undergone external influence if the thoughts which we entertain are unrelated to internal demands, than if they are intimately connected with them. It seems to me that revelation is a miraculous intrusion into the regular order, whether of images or natural law, and not an intensification of it. Hepburn and Cassirer both emphasize that the impact and apparent invasion of our minds by an image is a better guarantee that it has a supernatural source.[32]

A similar trap to which the image-theologian and myth-hunter fall prey is to assume that the power of the myth or symbol in evoking and convincing guarantees the reality of its reference, just as the historical recurrence of a religious symbol does. However, the valid sceptical option to both conclusions is that the human constitution finds certain images congenial and certain emotional appeals convincing. Fascism certainly employs a wealth of evocative symbols to which the Nietzschian or libidinal desires in man eagerly respond; the effective employment of symbols is one of the primary propaganda devices. But we would not wish to claim that people are being made aware of a political paradise. Therefore, as we remarked earlier concerning poetic truth, the argument from the persuasive power or beauty of poetic images to the truth or goodness of a metaphysical system is quite untenable. Once theology abandons rational arguments and a degree of empirical verification to win its case, it cannot successfully substitute the recommendation of religious ideas through poetry. We might also recall our earlier remark that if we ascribe truth-value to everything of evocative, persuasive poetic value, we soon find ourselves with a mutually incompatible or inconsistent cluster of ideas, each possessing an equally valid aesthetic backing. On this reading Nirvana would have as great a claim upon our credibility as Heaven; Heraclitus's doctrine of mutability would have equal grounds of proof with the static universe doctrine of Parmenides.

For the reasons listed above, I believe we can safely conclude that the attempt to conceive of religious language as myth or image collapses. Religious language which is logically precluded from having metaphysical or ontological implications is hardly a theologically acceptable idea.

For our particular purposes it affords little help, for if we attempt to place God's commands in the category of myth, then we are committed to the assumption that its significance lies in the way in which it harmonizes man's relationship with the universe. The way of escape from the dilemma of theological naturalism which we have been examining stresses the uniqueness of God's commands; this position appears to show its kinship with numerous other myths which attempt to reconcile man with his environment. In addition we have suggested that the persistence or recurrence of a myth seems to point to its human origin rather than to its divine origin. If this is true then the uniqueness achieved by commands emanating from God would also be destroyed.

As far as the concept of image is concerned, we could conceive of divine commands under a master image of *Kingship* or something of that sort; however, all of the above remarks would be equally appropriate. It seems that neither concept provides a means of resolving our difficulties.

NOTES

Chapter VI

1. For example the thematic inconsistency in Shakespeare's Sonnet XIV could be compared with several acknowledged contradictions which occur between the Gospels.
2. A somewhat analogous position attempts to preserve the moral fabric of religious exhortations while dispensing with its alleged basis in deity. And Mathew Arnold would retain the religious system of morality while dispensing with its 'emotional touch', despite Hume's analysis of the way in which the will is influenced.
3. Murry, J. M., *Discoveries*, London, Jonathan Cape, 1924, p. 42. Cf. also Willey, B., *Nineteenth Century Studies*, London, Chatto and Windus, 1961, p. 11.
4. Lewis, H. D., *Morals and Revelation*, London, Allen and Unwin, Ltd. 1951, pp. 209-210.
5. Santayana, G., *Poetry and Religion*, New York, Macmillan and Co., 1916, p. 191.
6. Farrer, A., *The Glass of Vision*, London, Dacre Press, 1958, p. 129.
7. *Ibid.*, p. 126.

8. Farrer, A., *The Glass of Vision*, p. 127.
9. *Ibid.*, p. 127.
10. *Ibid.*, p. 94.
11. Joyce, J., *Ulysses*, London, Bodley Head, 1960, p. 1.
12. Joyce, J., *Finnegan's Wake*, London, Faber and Faber Ltd, 1939, p. 629.
13. Berdyaev, N., *Freedom and the Spirit*, London, Geoffrey Bles, 1935, p. 70.
14. Müller cites examples of stories that 'would make the most savage of Red Indians creep and shudder', such as the cannibalism of Demeter and Cronus, and the mutilation of Uranus.
15. Banier, A., *La Mythologie et les Fables Expliquées par l'Histoire*, Paris, Chez Briasson, 1739.
16. Aristotle, *Metaphysics*, trans. by W. D. Ross, Oxford, Clarendon Press, 1924, xi, 8, 19.
17. Reardon, B. M. G., 'Philosophy and Myth', *Theology*, Vol. LXV, No. 502 April, 1962, p. 134-5.
18. Schelling, F. W. J., *Philosophie der Mythologie*, Stuttgart und Augsburg, F. G., Cotta'fcher Berlag, 1857.
19. Schelling, F. W. J., *ibid.*, p. 216 ff. Cf. also Schröter, M., *Schellings Werts*, München, C. H., Bed und R. Didenbourg, 1928, pp. 431–755.
20. Berdyaev, N., *Freedom and the Spirit*, pp. 52–88.
21. For an excellent discussion on the element of time in myth consult Cassirer, E., *Language and Myth*, trans. by A. Langer, New York, Macmillan and Co., 1946.
22. Reardon, B. M. G., 'Philosophy and Myth', pp. 138–39.
23. *Ibid.*, p. 138.
24. *Ibid.*, p. 136.
25. I might add that Reardon would involve himself in a contradiction at this point. For according to Reardon's bifurcation between myth and science it would be self-contradictory to speak of the myths of science. Yet Reardon would want to speak in this way by virtue of his previous definition of myth as C. D. Broad, Stephen Toulmin and Sir James Jeans actually do. All of these men use *myths of science* to mean the husks of pre-scientific thought which find expression in dramatic language or the metaphysical presuppositions which transcend evidential confirmation.
26. Farrer, A. M., *The Glass of Vision*, Westminster, Dacre Press, 1948; *A Rebirth of Images*, Westminster, Dacre Press, 1949; *A Study in St Mark*, Westminster, Dacre Press, 1951; *St Matthew and St Mark*, Westminster, Dacre Press, 1953. Thornton, L. S., *The Common Life in the Body of Christ*, Westminster, Dacre Press, 1950; 'The Mother of God in Holy Scripture' in *The Mother of God*, ed. by E. L. Mascall, London, Dacre Press, 1951; *The Doctrine of Atonement*, London, The Unicorn Press, 1937.
27. Creuzer, F. J., *Symbolik und Mythologie der Alten Völker*, Leipzig, Carl Wilhelm Leske, 1822.

28. These are some of the 'master-images' used by Thornton in the work entitled *The Common Life in the Body of Christ*.
29. Cf. Joachim, H. H., *The Nature of Truth*, Oxford University Press, 1939; Blanshard, B., *The Nature of Thought*, London, Allen & Unwin Ltd, 1939.
30. Cleobury, F. H., *Christian Rationalism and Philosophical Analysis*, London, Jas. Clarke and Co. Ltd, 1959, pp. 104-5.
31. Lewis, H. D., *Our Experience of God*, London, George Allen and Unwin Ltd, 1959, p. 142.
32. Cf. Cassirer, E., *Language and Myth*, p. 60.

Chapter VII

THE 'LOGICAL PARALLELS' APPROACH TO RELIGIOUS LANGUAGE

A: LOGICALLY ANOMALISTIC LANGUAGE
AND ANALOGY

The entire line of approach which attempts to discern significant logical parallels between religious discourse and other types of discourse, in order to illuminate the meaning of religious language, could be pursued at much greater length. The literature on this subject is quite voluminous and seems to be steadily increasing as more theologians are converted to this linguistic enterprise.

One splinter school within this general movement examines religious language as the language of paradox, logical anomaly and self-contradiction, which nevertheless remains meaningful. In this school we might place individuals such as J. M. Crombie ('The Possibility of Theological Statements' in *Faith and Logic*, ed. by Basil Mitchell), J. H. Thomas (*Subjectivity and Paradox*), Ronald W. Hepburn (*Christianity and Paradox*),[1] A. Macintyre ('The Logical Status of Religious Beliefs' in *Metaphysical Beliefs*), and Sören Kierkegaard (*Fear and Trembling*). This is by no means an exhaustive list but only a representative sampling of individuals united by an interest in somewhat similar conceptions of religious language.

Another splinter group seems greatly concerned with the doctrine of analogy in regard to theological discourse. The following writers offer a particular kind of analysis of the nature of analogical thought and discourse: E. L. Mascall (*Existence and Analogy*), H. Lytthens (*The Analogy Between God and the World*), Dom Pontifex (*The Meaning of Existence*), Austin Farrer (*Finite and Infinite*), and G. P. Klubertanz (*St Thomas Aquinas on Analogy*). A slightly different interpretation of analogy is offered by D. M.

The 'Logical Parallels' Approach to Religious Language

Emmet (*The Nature of Metaphysical Thinking*), and J. Maritain and E. Gilson present a third interpretation.[2] (This list could also be greatly extended.)

However, I do not believe that we need examine these approaches, or others of this nature. Our scrutiny of the concepts of ineffability, poetic language, myth and image are adequate for our purposes. For we can now arrive at the following conclusions:

(*a*) Religious discourse either cannot be successfully conceived as logically parallel to or as a species of certain other types of discourse, e.g. attempted expressions of the ineffable, or (*b*) religious discourse in general can be illuminated by comparisons with other types of discourse (e.g. poetic expression), but the comparisons prove unhelpful in resolving our particular dilemma. (Myth and image concepts exhibit features of both categories and could be said to exemplify a third type.) It seems to me that comparing religious discourse with any of the other types of discourse listed previously, would involve us in one or the other (or both) of these difficulties. Therefore, the *logical parallels* approach does not seem to improve our position one jot.

I might add to tidy up point (*b*) that the justification for this category is listed at the end of Chapter VI, Part A. Let me repeat it briefly. When, in comparing religious discourse to another mode of discourse, we find that it possesses sufficient cognitive content to satisfy theological standards (to render God's commands informative), then it does not possess the uniqueness necessary to rendering moral judgements of God's commands inappropriate.

However, before proceeding with the solution which the writer endorses, let me offer a general criticism of this entire theological approach.

B: RELIGIOUS LANGUAGE: ITS LOGICAL BEHAVIOUR AND ONTOLOGICAL STATUS

I do not think that anyone would doubt that if the God of the Hebraic–Christian tradition exists, that He is an extraordinary being indeed, and that numerous varieties of logically odd language would be necessary to indicate His nature, e.g. logical anomalies, paradoxes, metaphors and myths, enigmas and antinomies, category-transgression, qualified models, etc. Theological utterances may not be meaningless because they employ what are considered *idiosyncratic* expressions (as the Positivists too readily assert), however, they might well be empty; they have a meaning just as *The first zebra on Mars* has a meaning; however, they may not possess a reference with ontological status.

It is not only a simple task to coin extensions of meaning for familiar terms, but it is even simpler to invent descriptive phrases or uniquely referring expressions (as above) which do not answer to anything. For as Professor Ryle points out in his example about Hillary, 'Meanings and phrases are not New Zealand citizens; what is expressed by a particular English phrase, as well as by any paraphrase or translation of it, is not something with lungs, a surname, long legs and a sunburnt face. People are born and die and sometimes wear boots; meanings are not born and do not die and they never wear boots—or go barefoot either. The Queen does not decorate meanings. The phrase *the first man to stand on the top of Mount Everest* will not lose its meaning when Hillary dies. Nor was it meaningless before he reached the summit.'[3]

In the same way we can stipulate fresh meanings to be appended to archaic religious expressions (fresh meanings gleaned from our logical parallels approach) and so long as we do not flagrantly violate logic or unduly strain conventional usage, do much to improve their meaning. However, we must not delude ourselves into thinking that we have shown that the object to which these new expressions refer is a real existent. Phrases like *that upon which man feels absolutely dependent* or the *wholely other* would remain in possession of meaning even if there were not a being on whom we were absolutely dependent or who was wholly other. (We have come so far from Russell's *Theory of Types* that we can even attempt to speak of meaningful nonsense!)

This is, of course, a fundamental metaphysical question; not one confined to the logical character of linguistic expressions or

The 'Logical Parallels' Approach to Religious Language

universes of discourse. The above-mentioned writers therefore cannot be condemned for failing to answer a question to which they did not address themselves, however, they could be judged culpable in not dealing with this first order issue prior to the second order inquiry. 'To demonstrate the existence of a logically odd language plays straight into the empiricist's hands: he only has to reply that it is not necessary to prove laboriously that languages exist which are logically *odd*, for he knows this by observation already; while further, it has not yet been shown that *this* language is about anything, and he simply does not believe that it is about anything. Unless we prove the existence of God at the start, in such a way as to demonstrate the necessity for a logically *odd* language, there is no answer to the modern philosopher.'[4]

I do not wish to belabour this elementary point, however, since it is frequently overlooked I would like to illustrate its force by a somewhat prolix example. It will not make any difference to the point of the example if I temporarily blur the distinction between theology and cosmology.

Let us suppose that the Greeks took a page from their mythology and became convinced that the entire universe was actually resting on the shoulders of Atlas. (This hypothetical situation is not as extravagant as it appears when we remember that Braithwaite contends that religious assertions are given imaginative backing by their association with *stories* [logically equivalent to novels and other purely fictitious narratives], and Macintyre alleges that religious assertions are *myths* although myths which contain not only *mythical* elements but factual assertions as well.) As a consequence certain expressions which referred to and illuminated this metaphysical *reality* would assume primary importance. One such stratum of discourse would be *relational* terms and expressions such as *under, above, below, on top of, beneath, lower than, underneath,* and what may be ambiguously labelled *support* terms such as *understructure, sub-stratum, foundation, resting-place.* Another area of language which would be elevated would be terms referring to the physical size and power of Atlas —terms such as *gigantic, mighty, unyielding, colossal, inexhaustible* and *massive*. Of course if the Greeks in this fictitious society were linguistically astute or empirically erudite, these terms would then undergo re-definition in order to shed their finite, literal, terrestrial meanings and assume grossly extended, stretched meanings more cogent and appropriate in relation to their metaphysical reference. Thus self-contradictions such as *the above, below which there is not anything*, might be considered admissible as more closely approaching Atlas's sophisticated status, or Kierkegaardian paradoxes such as *the eternally yet temporally positioned entity*.[5] Even logical *nonsense* like *the unsupported support* or *the exhausted inexhaustible* (when it is not equivalent to *the perpetually fatigued*) might be judged as possessing the proper internal logic necessary to convey this transcendent scheme.

With apologies to Ian Ramsey (whose account of the nature of religious language is praiseworthy on numerous counts), a metaphysician might well appear to elucidate the methodological system by means of which a *discernment-commitment* situation might be evoked, e.g. using *exhaustible* as a Model and *in* as a Qualifier. An analogy between poetry, images, myths and symbols on the one hand, and religious language on the other might be presented to illuminate the logical meaning of language referring to the Atlas-supported world, such that apparently absurd sentences were declared *enigmatic by excess of meaning* or nonsensical in the same way as poetic expressions are nonsensical.[6]

An exasperated segment of the believing community might even be moved to reject all attempts to characterize, confirm or examine the nature of the Atlas-supported universe. Some might adopt an approach similar to Rudolf Otto and claim that religious feelings engendered by the *numinous* metaphysical understructure, are essentially non-rational and cannot be theologically conceptualized.[7] Others of this mental bent would probably claim *a la* Wittgenstein, that the religious beliefs arising from an inexpressible, mystically perceived system, cannot be formulated into theological questions much less given answers.[8] And a third group might, with Barth, make the epistemological point that

The 'Logical Parallels' Approach to Religious Language

the essence of the theological or cosmological structure is *ungraspable*; it cannot be rationally demonstrated by natural theology but can only be bestowed by an act of transcendent and divine grace.[9]

Lurking off-stage, however, is the disquieting, recurrent doubt as to whether the universe is so structured that Atlas is bearing the world upon his shoulders! This question remains the central, persistent one rather than ancillary concerns such as whether it is consistent or coherent for a system so constructed to possess logically tortured language or to lack rational formulation altogether. 'A religion could be quite consistent or coherent and yet entirely false. Any number of systems of belief could be constructed, given some imaginative ability, which would all pass the coherence test but which could not all be true.'[10]

In an effort to avoid the appearance of censoriousness in regard to religious language, let me say that just as the meaningfulness of a stratum of discourse does not imply the objective reality of its reference, so the meaninglessness of a *universe of discourse* does not imply that the reality to which it points (however imperfectly) is an imaginative construct. Mascall once remarked that most of the tragedy of modern philosophy lies in the belief that having refuted the indefensible views about certain fundamental notions, it assumes the destruction of the notions themselves. The most that criticisms of this sort can do is to demonstrate that a particular account of, say, the logical nature of religious language is untenable.

I would ally myself with J. Macdonald Smith and Frederick Copleston[11] in maintaining that the demonstration of the existence and nature of a divine being (not necessarily by means of syllogistic proofs) by reference to which a particular logical type of language is justified, holds logical and methodological priority to a characterization of religious language. For it is hardly possible to be sympathetic towards, or even justly to analyse the logical status, of language referring to God without first being assured of His existence.

It must be remembered that those writers who deal with the logical status of religious belief, in order to elucidate the way in which religious utterances can be verified, are at best concerned with the meaningfulness of language (as conveyed by words, phrases or sentences) rather than the ontological status of its referent. Language can be understandable without referring to a real existent, however the question of whether there is real referent should be asked of theological assertions.

At worst the aforementioned writers do not even attempt to supply the meaning of the key terms under discussion, but only describe the conditions under which these terms can be significant. To offer comments concerning the use of language or the logical status or variegation of verbal expressions, is a more sophisticated, peripheral, and needless to say different activity from giving the meaning of a term. To say that the phrase *on the right hand of God* is being used metaphorically does not give us its meaning. In addition, an analysis of the use of a term or phrase fails to come to grips with the more fundamental question of whether it possesses a respectable logical status (e.g. *informative* instead of or as well as *emotive*), just as supplying the meaning of the term *God* hardly assures us of the objectivity of its referent. Quite obviously we cannot maintain that every word, noun, or even every grammatical subject of a sentence names or corresponds to an appropriate denotatum, for then we would have an overcrowded Platonic universe populated with triangles, unicorns, varieties of conjunctions and articles, and all classes of real and imagined entities, as Russell and Wittgenstein demonstrated. Ryle's criticism of Husserl and Meinong is precisely that they confused the meaning of an expression with its denoted entity—that they spoke as if the denizens of their Third Realm were Meanings. However, there is little point in showing that theological assertions possess an odd nature or to lay bare the rules governing the use of theological expressions without being convinced that the deity characterized objectively exists. In a manner which would make analysts nod in approval, we can expose the role which a theological expression is employed to perform or provide a list of rules for translating religious assertions into a recognizable form, but we must also demonstrate that its subject-matter corresponds to a real entity, that there is a Being corresponding to the

The 'Logical Parallels' Approach to Religious Language

idea of God. To use Ryle's distinction slightly anomalously to the way in which Ryle intended it, *knowing how* the rules controlling religious discourse function, or classifying the logically important forms which religious utterances can display, does not supply us with *knowledge that* a deity exists. It seems to me a distinctive virtue of Ramsey's book, *Religious Language* that it presents a system whereby one may move from *knowing how* to *knowing that*; the knowledge of a particular system or technique leads to an elicitation of a spiritual experience, the assurance of the divine character and reality. However, in the case of theological assertions I would say that both he and Ryle are mistaken in supposing that *knowing how* is logically prior to *knowing that*. This is natural theology with a vengeance.

This is a rather reactionary position prescribing that a question of the sort *What is X?* should be answered prior to a question such as *What is the logical status of terms referring to X?*, that ontological issues have priority over linguistic considerations. The modern objection to this position is that the problem of meaning must be settled, prior to an inquiry into metaphysical issues, for only then can we know what sort of entity it is that we are seeking. Before one can ascertain whether the adjectives *infinite*, *omnipotent*, or *eternal* fit anything or not, or before one can begin an investigation of the rational evidence for the existence of an entity possessing these attributes, one must know the correct meaning of these descriptive terms.

It seems to me that this position is only tenable if meaning is interpreted as something like *sufficiently clear meaning to define the definiens* and not necessarily *the precise meaning involved*. (It often seems that the objective intention of religious terms is being sought when knowledge of the principal characteristics involved in their conventional intention will suffice.) For example, if a question were posed such as *Are there wuzaboos on the African continent?*, it would be absurd to criticize the priority of an inquiry into the meaning of the term *wuzaboo*. However, it is equally preposterous to claim that the logical variegation of language referring to *wuzaboos* or the native's ordinary usages of the term must be exhaustively analysed before a safari can begin to search for one. We are as reprehensible in over-preparing for our journey to the extent that we never actually embark upon it as we are for throwing ourselves into the jungle without an adequate idea of the quarry we are pursuing.

Moreover, in the theological discourse we are not dealing with completely unknown terms like *wuzaboo* but with ordinary words which only require some clarificatory analysis to make them meaningful. I fail to see why a large bulk of disputation must occur over the logical status, meaning or application of religious terms in peripheral contexts when, by and large, what is needed for ontological or theological investigation is agreement over the meaning of these expressions in nuclear contexts. And this agreement is either present at the start or requires a fraction of the linguistic toil currently employed to expose their logical strata or meaning. Obviously theological assertions need to satisfy more than the minimal requirement for a significant descriptive statement, i.e. they need to show that they have cognitive meaning and are not pseudo-statements compatible with every other conceivable descriptive statement; however, a detailed type-classification hardly helps toward solving key theological issues.

Understanding the concept-governing rules of a conceptual system is nonetheless as important an endeavour in theological discourse as elsewhere. And what has been called *usage-reporting* is probably as worthwhile an enterprise as, for example, an analysis of how symbols represent reality. My criticism is that we are given more linguistic and analytic information than we need to know in order to attack theological issues. Furthermore, it is sometimes (erroneously) felt that linguistic scrutiny is not a vital mechanism of philosophy but its *telos* and that ontological questions are unreal.

Now I certainly would not want to go as far as Gellner and say that *exhibition-analysis*, i.e. the exhibition of the logical rules governing concepts, is trivial or irrelevant to any philosophical question. However, I am closer to Gellner's position than Wittgenstein's when the latter regards getting a clear view of the rules of language (*übersehen wollen*) as the only legitimate enterprise of philosophy.[12] And I am surely a considerable distance from

The 'Logical Parallels' Approach to Religious Language

A. J. Ayer[13] and Rudolf Carnap[14] in their *Verbalism* (to use a phrase of Duncan-Jones) which maintains that all philosophical problems disappear when the words or expressions employed in their formulation are rigorously clarified.[15] Historical precedents for the view here supported can be glimpsed at in St Thomas. It was necessary to St Thomas's theory of analogical predication to investigate the nature of the language used about God, to ask what *powerful* and *just* meant when attributed to deity; however, he examined the conventional usage of these words, not all similar words, and his aim was the solution of a metaphysical issue, not exhaustive logical classification. And Aristotle surely examined the meaning and implications of ordinary moral judgments, but he did so in order to create a synthetic moral system.

NOTES

Chapter VII

1. Hepburn is actually an analyst of this concept.
2. G. F. Woods in his book *Theological Explanation* devotes considerable space to the structure and logical possibility of analogical reasoning.
3. Ryle, G., 'The Theory of Meaning' in *British Philosophy in the Mid-Century*, ed. by C. A. Mace, London, Allen and Unwin Ltd, 1957, p. 245.
4. Smith, J. M., 'How Do We Prove That God Exists', *The Downside Review*, Vol. 79, No. 256, Summer 1961, p. 220. Cf. also Hepburn, R. W., *Christianity and Paradox*, London, Watts, 1958, p. 80.
5. Cf. Kierkegaard, S., *Concluding Unscientific Postscript*, trans. by D. F. Swenson, London, Humphrey Milford, 1941, p. 194–206.
6. Cf. Farrer, A., *St Matthew and St Mark* p. 11. Cf. also Farrer's *The Glass of Vision*, Dacre Press 1948, p. 42, and *A Rebirth of Images*, London, Dacre Press, 1949, p. 18. R. W. Hepburn, 'Poetry and Religious Belief', in *Metaphysical Beliefs*, ed. by A. Macintyre, London, S.C.M. Press, 1957, pp. 85–166. Thornton, L. S., *The Dominion of Christ*, London, Dacre Press, 1952, pp. 9 ff. Williams, D. D., *Interpreting Theology*, London, S.C.M. Press, 1953, *passim*, exp. pp. 34 ff.
7. Cf. Otto, R., *The Idea of the Holy*, London, Oxford Univ. Press, 1923, *passim*, esp. pp. 1–41.
8. Cf. W. Wittgenstein, L., *Tractatus Logico-Philosophicus*, London, Kegan Paul, Trench, Trübner & Co., 1922, 6.44 – 6.522.

9. Cf. Barth, K., *Der Römerbrief*, München, Chr. Kaifer, 1926, p. 315.
10. Hepburn, R. W., *Christianity and Paradox*, London, Watts, 1958, p. 80.
11. Coppleston, F., *Contemporary Philosophy*, London, Burns and Oates, 1956, pp. 87–103.
12. Wittgenstein, L., *Philosophical Investigations*, trans. by G. E. M. Anscombe, Oxford, 1958, p. 50.
13. Ayer, A. J., *Language, Truth and Logic*, London, Victor Gollancz Ltd, 1936.
14. Carnap, R., *Logical Syntax of Language*, London, Kegan Paul, Trench, Trübner & Co., Ltd, 1937.
15. Cf. 'Are all Philosophical Questions, Questions of Language?', a symposium by Stuart Hampshire, Austin Duncan-Jones and S. Körner, *Arist. Soc. Supplementary*, Vol. XXII, 1948.

Chapter VIII
'GOD IS GOOD': AN ANALYTIC PROPOSITION

A: THE ESSENTIAL GOODNESS OF GOD

Another approach to this dilemma has logical features in common with the *ontological proof* for the existence of God. When confronted with the dilemma, *Does God love an act because it is good or is an act good because God loves it?*, the religious person might respond by saying that this is a meaningless question. It is not meaningless because we are illegitimately demoting God to a human level, creating God in our own image as it were, or failing to recognize the unique logical status of deity, but because we are artificially constructing two mutually exclusive alternatives, where only one question exists. And this one question is perhaps worthy of the interrogatory character but not the puzzling quality which the word carries with it, because it is immediately answerable.

The argument supporting this solution is simply this: that any act which God commands is, *ipso facto*, good. An act is neither made good by God's commanding or loving it, nor loved or commanded by God on the basis of its objective value; for *good action* and *action willed by God* are inseparably intertwined. The interposition of a premise containing a moral assessment of God's character or conduct is inappropriate and superfluous. The concept of goodness is an integral and intrinsic constituent of the concept of God so that if we believe that God wills certain actions, it follows that these actions are necessarily good.

It does not follow from the validity of the claim that *whatever God wills is good* that *whatever is good is willed by God*. The latter proposition would only be true if the entire class of *good actions* were co-extensive with the class of *actions willed by God*. That is to

Deity and Morality

say, it would only hold true if there were not any good actions which were not also actions willed by God. (This would not imply that deity and the moral order were identical, for God's nature extends beyond the sphere of morality, e.g. in His creating force and sustaining power in the universe.)

The truth of the proposition *whatever is good is willed by God* would therefore depend upon the immanence, power, scope, knowledge, love and other indefectible qualities customarily ascribed to God. If God were tender-mindedly thought of as omnipresent, omniscient, omnipotent, etc., then the converse of the proposition *whatever God wills is good*, would be just as true. The word of God as revealed in Scripture has been taken to establish these attributes, if we generalize from the particular instances and contexts in which His revelation is embedded. (If we do not, we erroneously assume that God's will, semi-codified in Biblical ordinances, being appropriate only to the Romans, Greeks, Philistines, etc. of early history, does not pertain to problems peculiar to Atomic Age man.) However, if theological systems place some important limitations on God's supposedly perfect nature, claiming Him finite in, say, power or love or knowledge (as theories have claimed, for example, in attempting to resolve the problem of evil), then some good actions can be said to spring from sources other than that of God's will. Only some of the class of good actions would be actions willed by God, and would perhaps possess the added goodness engendered by God's willing them. This would make the moral order greater in scope than God's will, but it would not mean that it would occupy a metaphysically supreme position. On this reading, it still would not make sense to ask *Does God love an act because it is good?*, for this question presupposes that either God's will is dependent upon moral goodness or that moral goodness is a function of God's will; that God in His perfection always chooses to will that which is good, or that God's willing an act somehow imbues it with goodness.

To continue in this old-fashioned, metaphysical manner, an important implication which this stand would have to allow is that God's will and the moral order would be independent

'God is good': An Analytic Proposition

strands, although crossing and fusing at the juncture of (most) right actions. God's will would overlap the moral order in its other realms of application (e.g. creation, divine intercession, etc.) and the moral order would overlap God's will in some moral situations. The two classes would be independent, with different limits and a common area of their core; neither would be supreme or subordinate in relation to the other. This is, of course, a much weaker position that two totally independent provinces.

To the philosopher who reiterates the likely objection at this point, that in order to know that the commands of God are good we must judge them by an independent moral standard, the religious man will counter that a deliberate act of judgment is not logically necessary to the possession of the knowledge that God is good. Religion can and has achieved knowledge (not in the Kantian sense) and cognizance (not in the Spencerian sense) of this attribute by means of an immediate awareness of God's predicates, virtually unmediated[1] in its initial discovery by reflective assessment. This vital core of information (like knowledge of God's existence) did not proceed by some dialectical architectonic from a state of ignorance to the full realization of God's being and nature. It became known to man through revelation in one form or another or *immediate intuition*. If we first came to believe that God is good from syllogistic reasoning rationally establishing this *fact*, it would be practically unprecedented in theological history.

The rank and file Christian is made aware of this attribute of God and seldom attempts a self-satisfying rational demonstration of his beliefs. He may reflect or theorize in an unsystematic way about the nature of God, His relationship with humanity, etc., but he does not normally attain knowledge of any important aspect of God's being on the basis of induction or an analysis of certain configurations of experience. Those few religious men called theologians, who systematically apply themselves to this task, do so by way of *post hoc* justification or philosophical retrospection about that which they are well convinced is true. They do not engage in their task to validate or establish some theological conclusions. (In this respect the modern theologian resembles his mediaeval counterpart with the important difference that revelation is not inflexible to interpretation, and reason is viewed with greater regard in tempering revelation. However, the question of what would count against a religious belief is still hammering at all doors, with slightly lesser insistence upon those of natural theologians.) In the case of most major religions today, their common, indispensable core is the immediate experience of God, as dynamically reported by inspired mystics, messiahs, prophets or saints. It is such *divine encounters* which father and direct the subsequent erection of theological structures, and provide content material for eulogizing or carping philosophers. If numerous philosophers became discouraged, like Hume at efforts to discover a rational argument, which would lead to deity, perhaps they would have misunderstood the nature of their subject, and entertained erroneous expectations as to its logical behaviour.

This view seems to be skirting dangerously close to the edge of the religious 'howler', *believe and then you will know*—a prescription for an order of knowledge and a metaphysical priority which, if anything, ought to be reversed. However, the contention herein described would not be committed to this viewpoint and holds that knowledge and belief do not occur separately in any order, or even in a continuum, but simultaneously inundate the mind of the recipient just as auditory and visual images jointly assail the senses in synaesthetic poetry.

It is an entirely different matter when we speak of judgments about God as contrasted with knowledge or belief of Him—and I use the propositions *of* and *about* advisedly. For here judgments about God are seen to succeed direct knowledge or belief of Him. Not that a temporal factor is logically relevant here, for the human mind may arrive by an *a posteriori* argument at the knowledge of an *a priori* relation; the order of discovery or knowledge (*ordo quoad nos*) must be distinguished from the order of being or reality (*ordo per se*).[2] It is simply important to notice that knowledge and belief or *knowledge-belief* of God are of a different logical and epistemological nature than judgements about God.

'God is good': An Analytic Proposition

Therefore, to the contention of Nielsen (and numerous others) that we must logically be supplied with the proposition that *Whatever God wills is right* before concluding *X is right* from *God wills X*, we can reply that we actually have no need for this express moral judgment when immediate contact with God assures us of this truth. It is not that we have an enthymeme here, the concealed premise of which need not be dredged to the surface, but that the argument or thought is already complete without this rational judgement. Neither is it the case that the major premise of the syllogism is spiritually apprehended rather than the object of a moral judgement (for this would merely alter the epistemological character or form of the major premise without challenging the necessity of the logical sequence), but that it is superfluous to the certainty of the conclusion.

For those repelled by the odious ring of metaphysics in the foregoing remarks, let me put the matter in respectable propositional form: *God wills X* therefore *X is good* does not require the proposition *Everything God wills is good*, because the concept of God already embraces the notion of absolute goodness. *God is good* is on this reading an analytic proposition; its truth or falsity is discoverable through an analysis of the subject *God*. The predicate is actually unnecessary to a real or theoretical intelligence possessing a thorough understanding of the subject. For the idea distinctly expressed in the predicate was implicit (*a priori*) in the subject. In the case of a proposition such as *The cat is friendly*, two independent ideas are being linked together. Since the cat's attributes are established *a posteriori*, by independent means, it is *logically possible* in the full technical sense of the phrase, that the cat could be found to be anti-social.[3] In fact she usually is. However, since the attribute of goodness is intrinsic to the concept of God, it would be grossly self-contradictory to declare that God is not good.

One major criticism which such an analysis could bring down upon its head is that propositions, the subject of which is *personal*, do not lend themselves to analytic formulation. *God is good* being a member of this class of propositions which would include *Robert Graves is prolific*, '*Mozart is witty*' and *Hume is intelligent* is, like them, a synthetic proposition which cannot be moulded by any linguistic manipulations into an analytic shape. Sentences of a logical, mathematical, relational and tautological kind furnish the stuff out of which analytic propositions are made. The truth or falsity of these types of propositions depends solely upon the rules governing the correct use of their symbols;[4] the truth or falsity of *P* is a function of what *S* symbolizes. The utterance *An equilateral triangle is not equiangular* and the universal negative proposition *All baby cats are not kittens* are obviously self-contradictory in a way that 'Schweitzer is not sensitive' is not self-contradictory—although it may not be true.

B: CONNOTATION AND DENOTATION

The controversy as to the possibility of personal sentences ever being analytic is intimately connected with the question of whether proper names have connotation. Admittedly most proper names do denote something in the real, or actual world, the exception being descriptive names such as *Apollo* and *Jean Valjean*, which Boole[5] and de Morgan[6] maintain have application in a particular mode or *universe of discourse*, very like Wittgenstein's *area of discourse* for mnemonics. Bertrand Russell is of course responsible for showing how *definite descriptions* which describe nothing (e.g. *The Queen of Switzerland*) can still be significantly employed. However, the question with which we are here concerned is whether *Jane*, *Nigel* or *Alison* have connotation as well as denotation or *extension*. Do these names serve no other function than denoting as Mill presupposed when he labelled proper names *unmeaning marks*?[7] Are proper names 'the only names of objects which connote nothing?'[8]

It will clarify our problem if we bear in mind Dr Keynes's classification of connotation into '*Conventional intension* . . . those attributes which constitute the meaning of a name; *subjective intension* . . . those (attributes) that are mentally associated with it, whether or not they are actually signified by it; *objective intension* or *comprehension* will include all the attributes possessed in common by all members of the class denoted by the name.'[9] For with this analytic scheme in mind we can detect at least one

'God is good': An Analytic Proposition

type of intension or connotation in a proper name—the *subjective intension* or psychological meaning of the word. Proper names do forcefully conjure up or evoke psychological meanings, images or associations in different people's minds. *Marx, G. B. Shaw, Wellington* and *St Francis of Assisi* are far from being sterile, disembodied labels; when understood to be the marks of certain individuals, we would want to say that they do possess connotation in at least a subjective sense. *Marx* calls to my mind intensity and misplaced dedication, *Shaw*, wittiness and Nietzschian iconoclasm, *Wellington*, tactical shrewdness and (as one philosopher has remarked) an aquiline nose, and *St Francis*, gentleness of spirit. Some of these characteristics may also be the comprehension of the above proper names, but that is getting ahead of ourselves. From this analysis we can at least understand Eaton when he writes that: 'When logicians insist that proper names are connotative, they usually mean that they carry a subjective intension with them.'[10]

As far as objective intension is concerned, this is an unworkable concept in every context including that of proper names, because human beings in their finitude never know all the attributes possessed by an object. This category thus has some theoretical application, but it does not possess utilitarian value since the complete set of properties comprising the objective intension can be infinite in number. Neither historians nor theologians would want to say that the objects of their studies have been exhaustively characterized. *God* and *Wales* are open-ended labels —both include qualities which have not been discovered. Still, if most proper names, including *God*, were found to possess connotation at all (excluding the subjective intension sense), then God would in principle possess objective intension as well as conventional intension. I might add in passing that God, being the only entity in the universe to which omniscience is ascribed, would be the only entity with complete cognizance of the objective intension of the word *God*—the only being with exhaustive self-knowledge.

Leaving *subjective intension* and *objective intension* in the wake of our inquiry, let us now turn to the logically important part of names, their *conventional intension*. It is vital to the achievement of our entire ends to examine this notion, because we are now in a position to see that the question *Do proper names have connotation?* is *Do proper names have conventional intension?* Only if proper names possess connotation in this sense can they be formed into *essential propositions*. And only if proper names in general (and *God* in particular in its usage as a member of this class) do possess conventional intension, can we regard some sentences with singular name subject, *is* of attribution copulas, and quality predicates, as analytic in form. For only then can the *quality* predicate be necessary to the *personal* subject.

The interpretation of connotation as conventional intension is certainly the one which Mill intended, when he claimed proper names to be destitute of connotative meaning. Mill's view is lucidly and succinctly put in the following passages: 'Proper names are not connotative: they denote the individuals, who are called by them; but they do not indicate or imply any attributes as belonging to those individuals. When we name a child by the name Paul, or a dog by the name Caesar, these names are simply marks used to be made subjects of discourse. It may be said, indeed, that we must have had some reason for giving them those names rather than any others; and this is true; but the name, once given, is independent of the reason. A man may have the name John, because that was the name of his father; a town may have been named Dartmouth because it is situated at the mouth of the Dart. But it is no part of the signification of the word John, that the father of the person so called bore the same name; nor even of the word Dartmouth, to be situated at the mouth of the Dart . . . Proper names are attached to the objects themselves, and are not dependent on the continuance of any attribute of the object.[11]

'When we predicate of anything its proper name; when we say, pointing to a man, this is Brown or Smith, or pointing to a city, that is York, we do not, merely by doing so, convey to the reader any information about them, except that those are names. By enabling him to identify the individuals, we may connect them with information previously possessed by him; by saying,

'God is good': An Analytic Proposition

This is York, we may tell him that it contains the Minster. But this is in virtue of what he has previously heard concerning York; not by anything implied in the name. It is otherwise when objects are spoken of by connotative names. When we say, The town is built of marble, we give the hearer what may be entirely new information, and this merely by the signification of the many-worded connotative name, 'built of marble'. Such names are not signs of the mere objects, invested because we have occasion to think and speak of these objects individually; but signs, which accompany an attribute; a kind of livery in which the attribute clothes all objects, which are recognized as possessing it. They are not mere marks, but more that is to say, significant marks; and the connotation is what constitutes their significance.'[12]

The view that there is no such thing as the connotation of a proper name, that proper names are 'the only names of objects which connote nothing', is echoed by a number of eminent and responsible logicians. For example, Bain remarks, 'As a mere mark, a name has no power beyond simply denoting, or pointing out its object; Sirius suggests the star of that name; London has no other function than to make us think of the object named.'[13] A. C. Mace in contrasting proper names with general names classifies proper names as being 'devoid of connotation, and not capable of use in conjunction with applicatives'.[14] And Whateley states: 'A term which merely denotes an object without implying any attribute to that object is called "*Absolute*" or "*Non-connotative*"; as "*Paris*" and "*Romulus*". The last terms *de*note . . . but do not . . . *con*note (imply in their signification) any attributes of those individuals.'[15] Fowler contradicts himself about this issue, first denying that words like Socrates are connotative, then affirming that of all words they are 'largest in connotation' and 'smallest in denotation'.[16] Finally, Keynes states categorically, 'A proper name is a name assigned as a mark to distinguish an individual person or thing from others, without implying in its signification the possession by the individual in question of any specific attributes.'[17]

Such is the traditional view and those logicians claiming that proper names do possess connotation must do so by means of a revolt or reaction against the *status quo*.

One weak mode of rescue for the revolutionists is to claim that every proper name is connotative by virtue of the fact, by analytic necessity, it implies individuality, and what is here important, the quality of being called by that name. Everything to which we assign a proper name, from dogs to dolls, must at least possess the connotation of being called by that name. Keynes outlines this position as follows: 'If we call a man John when he really passes by the name of James, we make a mistake; we attribute to him a quality which he does not possess—that of passing by the name of John.'[18]

In the first place it is important to notice that *quality* is being used in a strained sense so as to include *being called by that name* along with *large, equilateral, parent, just*, etc. In this light it is highly doubtful whether *being called by that name* is a quality of *hydrogen sulphide* or *John*.

In general, however, we must reply with Keynes that it is 'one thing to say that the identity of the object called by the name with that to which the name has previously been assigned is a condition essential to the correct use of a proper name, and another thing to say that this is connoted by a proper name. If indeed by connotation we mean the attributes by reason of the possession of which by any object the name is applicable to that object, it seems a case of ὕστερον πρότερον to include in the connotation the property of being called by the name.'[19]

Another argument which we can thrust aside is that which demonstrates the connotation of proper names by reference to expressions such as *a Caesar, a Gulliver, a Goliath, an Einstein*, etc. The inference here is that a certain type of individual is designated which (undeniably) possesses a conventionally assigned set of attributes. This argument will not do for the simple reason that although the names retain the appearance of being proper, i.e. maintain their overt grammatical structure, they have in this context altered their logical character. They have in fact become *general names* logically identical in this respect with *rock, governor*, and *painting* (Prof. Bain notwithstanding).[20] The somewhat

'God is good': An Analytic Proposition

paradoxical appearance is unmasked when we consider *amphibean* terms like *Quixotic*, *Keynesian* and *Socratic* which appear to breathe the air of two realms, but logically belong in the land of adjectival general names.

It would be appropriate to recall to mind at this juncture that the term *God* which this entire section is aiming towards characterizing, is a singular term in the monotheistic Hebraic-Christian tradition. We are not interested in the general name *god* referring to the deity which has been worshipped, anthropomorphically, animistically, polytheistically, etc. by primitive or primeval religions.

Let me say further that *God* as we are dealing with the term is not an individualization of the general term *god* which could be equally designated by a demonstrative pronoun or a definite article (e.g. this god or the god), but is a singular name which refers to a unique corresponding object. Like other singular names, it fails to meet a necessary criterion of general names—that *all* or *some* are potentially able to be meaningfully prefixed to it. However, whereas most members of the class of singular names gain their uniqueness from a specific limitation in time and/or space, e.g. the equator, the moon, etc., God achieves this specificity by virtue of his exemption from the limitations of time and space. This does not make the logical distinction between singular and general names inapplicable to *God*; this term is clearly within the singular name category but gains its inclusion by virtue of another sort of uniqueness to the corresponding object —namely freedom from terrestrial fetters of (among others) a spacio-temporal sort.

Conceiving the term *God* as a singular name does not, of course, exclude it from possessing connotation. For if we follow Mill's tripartite classification of names, we see that some singular names, irrespective of their degree of individualization, are acknowledged as being connotative.

To return to the main thread of our discussion, it can be seen that none of the answers put forward in this section will quite do. However, I believe that proper names legitimately can be said to connote for the reasons discussed in the next chapter.

NOTES

Chapter VIII

1. It is unnecessary to quibble about whether human beings as finite creatures are precluded from gaining totally unmediated contact with God as H. D. Lewis (*Our Experience of God*, London, Allen and Unwin Ltd, 1959, Ch. 1 and p. 284) and others have proclaimed, or whether God's transcendent nature somehow necessitates unmediated *confrontation*. The important element to notice is that reasonable judgement is never assumed to be the essential or initial epistemological channel to God.
2. H. B. Jevons entire discussion on whether morality is based on religion or vice versa, by reference to which occurred first in the history of religions, is vitiated by his failure to take cognizance of this logical point. Cf. Jevons, H. B., *An Introduction to the Study of Comparative Religion*, New York, The Macmillan Co., 1908, pp. 211–39.
3. A less easily pigeon-holed sentence would be *Gold is incapable of volatilization*, for the following reasons. If the chemists discovered a metal which resembled gold in every respect, that is, was characterized by its non-liability to rust, metallic lustre, yellow colour, high specific gravity, and great malleability and ductility, yet was *capable* of volatilization, would this metal deserve the name *gold*? Those who would opt for its being *gold*, with the addition of a property previously undiscovered, would in fact be interpreting *Gold is incapable of volatilization* as a synthetic proposition. On the other hand, those who declared that it was a new metal which bore a strikingly high degree of similarity to *gold*, would be interpreting *Gold is incapable of volatilization* as an analytic proposition. Such cases are of a borderline nature and illuminate the imperfections of a strict analytic synthetic duality. For they can be whipped in either direction depending upon the interpretation adopted. For further discussion concerning the fluid, dynamic nature of the analytic synthetic duality consult Bradley, F. H., *Principles of Logic*, Oxford, 1922, Vol. 1, p. 172; Veitch, J., *Institutes of Logic*, Edinburgh, Wm. Blackwood and Sons, 1885, p. 237; Keynes, J. N., *Formal Logic*, London, Macmillan and Co., 1906, pp. 53–5; Joseph, H. W. B., *An Introduction to Logic*, Oxford, University Press, 1946, pp. 207–15; Lotze, H., *Logic* trans. by B. Bosanquet, Oxford Univ. Press, 1887, pp. 84, 91.
4. Dr J. N. Keynes has suggested another type of analytic expression 'formal propositions' such as 'An animal is an animal'; propositions of this sort 'are valid whatever may be the meaning of the term involved . . .' 'their validity is determined by their bare form'. Keynes, J. N., *op. cit.*, p. 52. Sigwart also discusses this tautological type of analytic proposition: Sigwart, C., *Logic* trans. by H. Dendy, New York, Macmillan and Co., 1895, p. 86.

5. Boole, G., *Laws of Thought*, London, Walton and Maberley, 1854, pp. 46, 52, 176.
6. De Morgan, A., *Formal Logic*, ed. by A. E. Taylor, London, The Open Court Co., 1926, pp. 41, 55.
7. For excellent discussions on the way in which proper names do and do not signify real objects see Braithwaite's article and Moore's article in 'Imaginary Objects', *Arist. Soc. Suppl.*, Vol. XII, 1933, pp. 44-54 and 55-70, respectively.
8. Mill, J. S., *A System of Logic*, London, Longmans, Green, Reader & Dyer, 1870, Vol. I, p. 36.
9. Keynes, J. N., *Formal Logic*, p. 27.
10. Eaton, R. M., *General Logic*, New York, C. Scribner's and Sons, 1931, p. 246.
11. Mill, J. S., *A System of Logic*, pp. 33-4. I might insert at this point that the reason for a name being given to an individual or object is not the same as the reason why a word became a name.
12. *Ibid.*, p. 37.
13. Bain, A., *Logic*, London, Longmans, Green and Co., 1879, Part I, p. 49.
14. Mace, C. A., *The Principles of Logic*, London, Longmans, Green and Co., 1933, p. 85.
15. Whateley, R., *Elements of Logic*, London, John W. Parker, 1868, 9th Ed. pp. 122-3.
16. Fowler, J., *Deductive Logic*, Oxford Univ. Press, 1867, pp. 20-2.
17. Keynes, J. M., *op. cit.*, pp. 13-14.
18. *Ibid.*, p. 47.
19. Keynes, J. M., *Formal Logic*, p. 47.
20. Bain, A., *Logic*, pp. 48, 49.

Chapter IX

THE CONNOTATION OF PROPER NAMES

A: PROPER NAMES AND DESCRIPTIVE TERMS

Let us attack the problem afresh in this section by quoting Venn's well-known statement: 'I find in a parish register an entry of the burial of *John Thistlewaite Barker, farrier*: what sort of information can we extract from this bare description?' Venn goes on to answer that claiming from this 'bare designation' anything except that the individual referred to shoes horses 'involves at most a violent presumption'.[1]

Now against this view it could be maintained that we can determine several attributes from this proper name, without even knowing the specific person to whom it refers. For one thing, we could be reasonably sure that the term refers to a male human being. The name John could be applied to a bird, an automobile, a woman, or even a ship (if we chose to ignore maritime tradition), but all of these usages are strained extensions of that name normally given to male individuals. When *John* is applied to objects or female persons, an explanation in some form is appropriate to account for this unusual use of an ordinarily straightforward term. (A measure of the need for an explanation could be found in the surprise registered by an individual at learning the referent of the proper name.) That is, the need for an accompanying explanation would be in direct proportion to the departure from common usage, e.g. when the name John was applied to a piece of broken glass, a shaft of sunlight, an historical event, a book-end, a cumulus cloud, etc., an explanation of this peculiar usage is strongly demanded. To alleviate an uninitiated person's mystification or misinterpretation we ought to supply a full verbal explanation such as: *We call that shaft of sunlight that filters through the french doors at ten o'clock on summer mornings* John, *because it arrives at the same time that he usually does*, or *I call that cumulus cloud* John *because it pictorially objectifies his buoyant, serene disposition*. However, it would still be appropriate to offer some explanation of our verbal behaviour when we use language in a less unconventional way such as in calling a ship *John*. We might explain this '*rara avis in terris*' by reference to the fact that the owner of the vessel is a mysogynist, or that he does not believe in any exceptions to the grammatical rule of English that places or things are of neuter gender. In any case, since calling things other than male human beings by the name of *John* is contrary to our expectations, an explanation of the extended usage is logically appropriate. In the absence of an explanation or some warning sign preparing those concerned for the oddity of language, it bears a high degree of probability that *John* designates a male human being.

Now it is quite obvious that linguistic usage cannot be legislated to ensure a uniform expectation. That is to say, we cannot demand that an explanation be provided at every extraordinary or unusual employment of a proper name in the interest of cognitive clarity. The above remarks are not intended to foster any such linguistic revolution. What I hope they have shown is that the measure of the *unconventionality of meaning* can be ascertained by the need for explanatory remarks to avert misinterpretation; and that the common, ordinary reference which we are entitled to expect of a proper name (because of its great frequency of occurrence) is that of a human being—a human being with certain consequent characteristics.

I said *with certain consequent characteristics* quite advisedly because, from the fact that the label *John* refers to a human being, we can determine such things as his mental capabilities—e.g. that he is capable of using language, abstract thinking, imagining, reflecting, learning from experience (as contrasted with responding to conditioning), emphasizing, willing, etc.; physical structure and skills, e.g. that he is an erect biped, capable of locomotion, with opposable thumb and forefinger, warm blood, complex cerebral cortex, etc.; and organic needs, e.g. that he inhale oxygen, nitrogen and carbonic acid gas and exhale carbon dioxide, that he maintain a certain nutritional balance between carbohydrates, protein, fat, minerals and vitamins, that he sleep a minimum of five hours in every twenty-four, that he maintain a body temperature of close to ninety-eight and four-tenth degrees and so on.

From the fact that he is a male human being we can be assured that he exhibits further characteristics of a physiological, anatomical, and perhaps a dispositional sort (although cross-cultural studies leave this last category quite problematic). That is to say, we can establish his high proportion of muscular tissue, his glandular pattern and composition, reproductive organs, skeletal structure, proportion of subcutaneous fatty tissue, and perhaps his propensity toward active rather than sedentary (passive) activities. (This last item is derived from the fact that men carry the bulk of their weight in the upper part of their torsos, unlike women who have the major concentration of weight in the lower half of their bodies.)

In addition to our being reasonably certain that John Thistlewaite Barker is a human being, and, more specifically, a male human being, we are also justified in assuming that he is of English background, just as we might claim that *Juan Fernandez* is of Spanish stock, *John Johnson* is of Norwegian extraction and *Yung Cheng* is of Chinese descent. The current nationality of the above-mentioned individuals would be somewhat more indeterminable in an age when nationalities and indigenous names are able to be discarded or assumed without insuperable difficulty. However, it is quite probable that Juan Fernandez is a Mediterranean type with such anatomical characteristics as short stature, large nasal index, slight build, dark skin, black eyes and hair, and narrow head (dolichocephalous); that John Johnson is a Nordic type with white skin, blonde hair, blue eyes, tall stature, small nasal index, bony frame, narrow head and curly hair (cymotrichous); and that Yung Cheng is a Proto-Malay type with yellow skin, black hair and eyes, short stature, slight build, small nasal index, prominent cheekbones, flattened face and round head (brachycephalous).

The Connotation of Proper Names

Finally, from their nationalities we would even be able to determine something about their character. For, we must allow that their respective characters were predominantly shaped by environmental influences within the framework of their national cultures. That is, the nations of which they are members have provided the possibilities of development among which they have unconsciously been formed or consciously made their choice. They have definitely been unconsciously influenced by numerous physical factors such as their respective nation's size, shape, outline, geographical position, atmosphere, climate, density of population, age distribution, male to female ratio, and principal vocation (i.e. whether pastoral, industrial or agricultural). In addition, their characters have also been formed by acquiescence to (as well as reaction against) their respective nation's family pattern, dress, concept of beauty, recreation, ornamentation, moral code, language, religion, class structure, political system, literature, law, education, etc. If as great a heterogeneity of beliefs, temperament, outlook, disposition, opinions, etc., existed within, say, Spain as exists between China and Spain, then there would not be a phenomenon such as national character which proceeds from all of the above elements peculiar to a given country. The character of the individual as a microcosm of the national character will certainly vary but within specifiable limits; it will vary in the same way as individual figures vary within the confines of statistical averages. It is in recognition of this fact that William James speaks of living or dead options. 'A living option is one in which both hypotheses are live ones. If I say to you: *Be a theosophist or be a Mohammedan*, it is probably a dead option, because for you neither hypothesis is likely to be alive. But if I say: *Be an agnostic or be a Christian*, it is otherwise: trained as you are, each hypothesis makes some appeal, however small, to your belief.'[2]

The cultural and physical environment of a nation therefore provides the limits within which the mental attitudes, beliefs and ideas of individual characters develop. Ruth Benedict's famous book *Patterns of Culture* makes the trenchant point that various peoples have made different selections out of the multitudinous array of ways of living, and have woven them together into integrated patterns of culture. Miss Benedict may have gone astray in allowing a greater degree of conscious choice and free-will exercised by a society in this process than is actually involved, however it remains true that the particular selections which are made. and the relative importance which is attached to different ways of life, gives the group its characteristic pattern and serves to differentiate its members from those of other cultures. 'No man ever looks at the world with pristine eyes. He sees it edited by a definite set of customs and institutions and ways of thinking . . . The life history of the individual is first and foremost an accommodation to the patterns and standards traditionally handed down in his community. From the moment of his birth the customs into which he is born shape his experience and behaviour. By the time he can talk, he is the little creature of his culture, and by the time he is grown and able to take part in its activities, its habits are his habits, its beliefs his beliefs, its impossibilities his impossibilities. Every child that is born into his group will share them with him, and no child born into one on the opposite side of the globe can ever achieve the thousandth part."[3]

The implications of this theory espoused by Ruth Benedict, Margaret Mead, Gregory Bateson, Julian Blackburn, Otto Klineberg and others, is that the cultural pattern will in most cases be the predominating force in moulding the individual over any innate, congenital differences which he possesses.

Insofar as every individual is born into a nationality and will speak the native language (cognitively assimilating its conceptual framework), wear the expected clothes, and have a propensity toward emulating the group virtues (or reacting against them), etc., etc., his character is determinable. A generalization or a *stereotype* of different characteristics of different nations is more than likely to be influenced by personal bias and prejudice. However, the scientific and historical study of a national culture can lead us to certain safe conclusions about the individuals within that community. In Venn's example of *John Thistlewaite Barker* we can at least expect with a high degree of probability that he will revere honesty more than treachery (unlike the Dobu

The Connotation of Proper Names

Islanders), worship Christ sooner than Buddha, formulate and express his thoughts in English not Swahili, wear trousers not a loin cloth, favour monogamy over polygamy, love his mother more than his uncle, prefer democracy to fascism or timocracy, think belching is impolite rather than complimentary, exalt the virtues of football over those of baseball, regard white skin as lovelier than yellow skin, etc. At some points we would be able to ascertain his preferences (and ultimately his character which proceeds from his thoughts and actions) with a high degree of probability; at others, only the range within his predilections will vary.

Let us now recapitulate our thesis. We have said that from the bare designation *John Thistlewaite Barker* we are able to determine certain factors without even knowing the denotation of the proper name. We can safely assume that this label refers to a human being, of the male sex, and of English nationality. From the fact of his being a human being we know that he possesses certain mental capabilities, a specifiable physical structure and group of skills, some innate organic needs, etc. From the facts that he is a male human being we can be assured that he exhibits appropriate physiological, anatomical and perhaps dispositional characteristics. And finally, from his English nationality we can determine his race group and (perhaps) something about his character.[4]

I have further maintained that with a knowledge of each of these characteristics, certain other attributes can be seen to follow, e.g. his ability to use language, his warm bloodedness, his need for sleep, etc., which are consequent upon his being human; his proportion of muscular tissue, his knee structure, etc., which necessarily follow from his being a male member of the species; his having white skin, narrow head, etc., and his predilection for wearing trousers, expressing himself in English, etc., all of which are relative to his being of English nationality.

B: PROPER NAMES AND GENERAL MEANING

Critics of the preceding argument would probably want to put forward one or more of the following objections: Whereas

Deity and Morality

Yung Cheng can indicate an Oxford punt, or a female chimney sweep, or a Nordic Englishman who does not care a straw for either Buddha or Confucius, general concrete names like *tree, chair, ship* and *man* designate attributes which are fixed and universally common to those objects which they denote. We know that when the word *tree* is written or uttered that it connotes a woody, perennial plant with self-supporting stem or trunk, and so on; we are able to circumscribe a class of flora by virtue of these distinguishing attributes. In other words, whereas general concrete names like *tree* and *ship*, and even attributive terms like *short, conscientious* and *sickly* have a fixed general meaning, proper names like *John Barker* have not; although we have knowledge of the characteristics which any object legitimately labelled a tree will possess by virtue of the very meaning of the term *tree*, proper names can logically be applied to a variety of objects each with widely divergent attributes. Therefore proper names do not possess connotation.

Now if we maintained a position such as this, that because proper names do not have a fixed general meaning they are not connotative, on what presuppositions would this be founded? To my mind there is just one principal assumption:

We would be assuming that *fixed general meaning* is an essential attribute of *connotation*, such that any term which does not possess it is *ipso facto* excluded from the extensional class of connotative terms. In this case we would be making the statement: *All connotative terms have a fixed general meaning*, a true analytic proposition claiming that the characteristic of general meaning necessarily requires inclusion in the list of *characteristics of connotation* (in the connotation of *connotation*).

Now it is impossible to rely upon the designative meaning which *connotation* has in accepted usage to determine whether a fixed general meaning ought necessarily to be included in its conventional intension. This is the procedure adopted in constructing most analytic definitions, e.g. in a proposed analytic definition of the term *tool* it would be a serious departure from accepted usage if we excluded the quality of utility or the extensional referent of a hammer. Unfortunately, our task is not that

The Connotation of Proper Names

simple because there is a hesitation or doubt in common usage which permits inclusion or exclusion of *fixed general meaning* in the analytic definition of *connotation*. Fixed general meaning stands in relationship to the attributive term *connotation* as the extinct species Jamoytius stands to the general concrete name *vertebrate* or *virus* stands to the general concrete name *organic matter*. In the latter case, for example, the issue is in doubt because viruses assume perfect crystalline structures like other inorganic particles yet remain able to assume a condition in which division and multiplication is accomplished like living organisms. In the same way there is a doubt as to whether a fixed general meaning should be included or excluded from the definition of *connotation*. And this doubt is present because of the existence of proper names which exhibit significant characteristics of connotative terms, i.e. that numerous attributes are implied by the names, yet do not seem to possess a fixed general meaning.

All connotative terms have a fixed general meaning, might therefore be considered a borderline proposition capable of being considered true or false depending upon the meaning attached to the key term *connotation*—one which unfortunately fails to display a precise meaning in relation to the predicate.

However, it seems to me that the inexactitude does not merely leave the issue in an agnostic state of indecision, but is itself the deciding factor in concluding that *fixed general meaning* is *not* essential to the term *connotation*. It is only when the subject term upon analysis reveals a precise meaning in relation to the predicate, that we are justified in declaring that the predicate attribute is necessary to it.

In addition, just as the imprecise usage of *connotation* does not allow us to declare that the analytic proposition *All connotative terms have a fixed general meaning* is true, this same imprecision does not justify our declaring that this proposition is even analytic!

If we could legitimately declare that it is a true, analytic proposition that *All connotative terms have a fixed general meaning*, i.e. one in which the connection between the subject and predicate contained within is 'cogitated through identity', to use Kant's phrase,[5] then proper names which lack the predicate attribute

Deity and Morality

could not be included in the extensive meaning of *connotation*. However, if the predicate *fixed general meaning* is not found to be a necessary constituent of the subject term, then it is not a false analytic proposition, but a false *synthetic* one. And the synthetic proposition being false would mean that proper names are not excluded from the extensional meaning of *connotation* because they lack the predicate attribute.

In the latter case we can determine that the proposition is a *synthetic* one, at the same moment that we discover that a fixed general meaning is not an essential attribute of *connotation*. For when a predicate term is found to be inessential to the subject, then the proposition in which it is contained is not a false analytic proposition but not an analytic proposition at all. Furthermore, we can determine that it is a *false* synthetic proposition at the same moment that we conclude it is not an analytic one. Because we reached this conclusion by virtue of an examination of the common meaning of *connotation*, we should have to adopt the same procedure in deciding upon its truth or falsity as a synthetic proposition. For the term *connotation* is neither a concrete general term nor an attributive term which has a strong empirical grounding like *horse* or even *polite*, such that we could conduct a scientific investigation or empirical examination to determine whether certain characteristics are in fact common to the designated objects or qualities. *Connotation* is rather an epiphenomenal term (if you will), like *synonym*, *category* or *sentence*, which serves to classify language from a particular direction. It is expressive of a formal scheme which can be laid over linguistic expression in the interest of grammatical and logical illumination. It endeavours to do justice to a segment of the structure and complexities of language—to provide a useful tool by the manipulation of which order and insight may be gained. As a word of this nature, the ordinary verbal employment of *connotation* must be examined in determining its logical structure. This is, in fact, the procedure which we employed when we considered it as the subject term of the supposedly analytic proposition, *All connotative terms have a fixed general meaning*, and found that general meaning was not essential to its definitive meaning. (I might add somewhat paradoxically, that the general meaning of *connotation* is not deficient for lack of *general meaning* either.) Therefore it will serve as a basis for the conclusion that this proposition is false when considered as synthetic in nature.

For the above reasons I believe that connotation cannot be withheld or denied to proper names on the basis of the supposedly essential connection which fixed general meaning bears to connotation.

Having discussed and refuted this major criticism, let us turn to several minor criticisms directed against a term possessing connotation without possessing general meaning.

A seemingly fundamental criticism which arises out of the foregoing remarks is that once you have extracted from connotation the qualities of being fixed and generalizable the concept ceases to have meaning. In other words, if we define connotation in the way that Keynes does as 'the attributes by reason of the possession of which by any object the name is applicable to that object'[6] we are forced to allow that the meaning attached to a name enables the name to be generally applied to all objects of which the meaning is true. If we deny the latter then we make nonsense of the former.

There are two replies to this. One is to point out that the sort of definition of connotation which Keynes and numerous others put forward has the concept of fixed general meaning already built into it. Connotation implies generalizability by definitions of this sort. However it need not do so and as I have argued it should not do so. An example of a definition of connotation in which the concept of general meaning is excluded would be 'the meaning which the name implies, in contrast with (denotation) considered as the whole range of individual objects or instances to which the name applies.'[7] *All connotative terms possess attributes* is a valid analytic proposition, whereas *All connotative terms possess fixed general meaning* is not. By following the former analytic definition of connotation rather than the latter, non-essential one, we can see that proper names are clearly admissible and that the concept of connotation is not drained of meaning.

However, if this solution is unacceptable, perhaps because it is regarded as arbitrary and not in full accord with common usage or a lexical definition, or the reader suspects that the procedure employed to demonstrate that fixed general meaning is not necessary to connotation is a dubious one, then perhaps the following solution to our difficulties will prove more acceptable.

If it were, in fact, true that all connotative terms were applicable to more than one object by virtue of their intensional meaning, that still would not exclude proper names from being connotative. For if our analysis is correct, whereby we showed that numerous attributes are implied by proper names, then these attributes might also be regarded as *generalizable*. They would be the attributes by reason of the possession of which by any object the name is *appropriate* to that object. Schiller states 'it is a peculiarity of proper names that when they are thus transferred from one individual to another their meaning changes *totally*. A similar transfer of a common term hardly seems to affect its meaning at all. When *man* is transferred from Tom to Dick, a solid nucleus of common *humanity* in both seems to survive the change.'[8] However, we have seen that when *Juan Fernandez* is transferred from one object to another we can expect both objects to be male human beings, of Mediterranean race type, etc. It would be an inappropriate violation of the meaning involved, a serious departure from common usage, although not logically unsound, to apply this proper name to a Nordic Englishman. As we mentioned previously, in order to prevent misunderstanding of meaning, this employment of the word ought to be avoided. And there is a sense in which the name is applied to an object by virtue of the attributes which it possesses; a way in which the proper name has fixed general meaning.

As we have seen, proper names do convey characteristics and are not purely arbitrary labels about which this could not be stated. In this respect they differ from prison or army numbers from which no information can be ascertained. Proper names are words which have a certain latitude of meaning, which sets them a few degrees apart from straightforward descriptive terms; however, they also possess a descriptive content which limits their application. For proper names are not simply a jumble of letters in a social vacuum, but a meaningful arrangement of vowels and consonants firmly rooted in a social context. It is this social context which constitutes its descriptive foundation and limits the range of objects to which the proper name can be appropriately applied.

In fact, although we argued at great length that proper names could be connotative without possessing fixed general meaning, a strong case could be drawn up for saying that proper names do possess fixed general meaning. For proper names do embody the descriptive elements previously mentioned and hence do have limits to their application; they are not so vague as to be precluded from possessing fixed general meaning.

Of course one of the principal differences which marks off descriptive terms from proper names is that certain sentences containing descriptive terms can be self-contradictory, whereas sentences containing proper names (as subjects or objects) can never be called self-contradictory. For example *Some fathers do not have children* is patently absurd, whereas *Yung Cheng is Caucasian* is logically possible. However, the descriptive framework underlying the proper name *Yung Cheng* would make the term inapplicable (in the sense of misleading and hence logically inappropriate) to a Caucasian. Precisely insofar as proper names possess descriptive meaning, springing from their social roots, they are applicable or inapplicable to a class of objects.

I doubt whether anyone would seriously maintain that only those words which could be employed in a self-contradictory manner possess general meaning. We might well declare that terms which have sufficient descriptive meaning to be inappropriately employed, are terms which have fixed general meaning as well.

Another criticism often made against the connotation of proper names centres around the vagueness which proper names exhibit. Although it is sometimes admitted that proper names do have a connotative range, its range is regarded as too wide and with too indefinite limits for inclusion in the connotative category.

Max Black's article 'Vagueness: An Exercise in Logical Analysis', takes the concrete noun chair and demonstrates its vagueness by virtue of the situations in which its application is *doubtful* or *ill-defined*. He quotes the remarks of H. G. Wells on the extraordinary variety of objects to which the word *chair* is applied—armchairs, thrones, dentist's chairs, opera stalls, kitchen chairs, etc. Then he remarks, 'The vagueness of the term chair is typical of all terms whose application involves the use of the senses. In all such cases, *borderline cases* or *doubtful objects* are easily found to which we are unable to say either that the class name does or does not apply.'[9] We would want to push this idea even further and declare as Bertrand Russell did in his article on vagueness, that 'all language is more or less vague'.[10] The fact that proper names have vague limits does not militate against their possessing connotation. We run a risk of error in the case of proper names and in the case of ordinary descriptive terms, particularly when either are employed in a strained sense, e.g. when *chair* is used to include a throne and *John Johnson* is used to refer to an African Negro. It may be argued that proper names intrinsically possess a propensity towards unhealthy elasticity and that extended uses occur more frequently among them. However this is a difference in degree and not in kind. And we certainly cannot deny connotation to proper names because odd usage does occur to stretch the normal meaning. The fact of vagueness seems totally irrelevant to the question of whether or not proper names possess connotation.

Following this point on vagueness it might be appropriate to add a note on ambiguity. I believe that the charge that proper names are so ambiguous that they cannot be regarded as connotative can be met on the basis of arguments listed in our discussion of fixed general meaning. However, there is another approach which tries to prove that proper names *possess* connotation by reference to a concept of ambiguity. I do not believe that this procedure leads to a valid conclusion.

A person endorsing this approach would formulate his argument in this way. The view that proper names are devoid of connotation turns upon the assumption that proper names are logically applicable to different objects, each with different characteristics. However, is this a case of ambiguity—ambiguity to which descriptive terms (which possess connotation) are also

The Connotation of Proper Names

prone? We would not wish to drum words like *foot, bar* and *bank* out of the corps of connotative terms because they are equivocal. It is, in fact, totally irrelevant to a term's possession of connotation, whether it has a dozen referents. All that is necessary in these circumstances is to learn each of the general meanings connoted by the term and, subsequently, the range of denoted objects.[11]

As indicated above, this approach does not attempt to abolish ambiguity in the interest of clarity but recognizes that it is a salient, necessary feature of language. It is recognized that common usage cannot be altered by legislation and that it would be inadvisable to do so; the limited number of words in a given language cannot be multiplied to cover an almost infinite number of referents without rendering the language entirely too cumbersome and unwieldy. Equivocation, therefore, is recognized as an intrinsic and beneficial element of language, enriching its poetry, facilitating its handling and decreasing its logical clarity.

However, advocates of this approach then attempt to explain the extreme number of referents for each proper name by labelling them homonyms, i.e. words having the same form yet a different sense. (The Greek word from which it is derived is homonumon, which adds weight to this analysis.) By this move, however, I do not see that anything is gained. Homonym is substituted for extreme ambiguity but it does not lessen the difficulties engendered by the attempt to illustrate that proper names are simply ambiguous. It still remains to be shown that the apparent difference in kind is actually a difference in degree.

I might insert at this point that when one is confronted with the difficulties engendered by the denotation/connotation distinction there is a disturbingly strong temptation to simply jettison these concepts altogether as an encumbrance. (For similar reasons Collingwood and Oakeshott advise abandonment of the concept of causation in historical contexts.) F. H. Bradley says, for example, that we ought to 'dismiss forever the term *connotation* and try to keep clear of the errors it beacons'.[12] Bradley would say that we ought to do this because denotation and connotation 'serve no useful purpose in logic. They are unnecessary and objectionable.'

In the light of our study we might find grounds for dispensing with connotation because it is too narrow to account for the fullness and variety of language; it might be said to create more difficulties than it eliminates by forcing us to cram ill-fitting terms into rigid conceptual moulds.

However, we would have a great deal of difficulty in purging logic of this general distinction (if we wished to do so) because the distinction indicated seems crucial to the logical nature of language. And we cannot eliminate these terms because as Joseph points out 'the jingle of the antithesis' and Mill's authority have combined to make these terms commonly acceptable. Also as Mill himself pointed out there is a certain grammatical mobility about the terms which enables us to use forms like *to denote* and *to connote*, or *connoting* and *denoting* which we are not able to do in the case of extension and intension. We would have far greater difficulty in dismissing the conceptual division altogether because it does not touch the essence of language at some vital points. In any case the distinction between connotation and denotation does not seem to justify the extravagant claims which have been made for it: that it is 'the most valuable distinction for purposes of intellectual profit to be found within the field of common logic', or 'one of those distinctions which go deepest into the nature of language', but it does seem a useful analytic tool to retain.

Let us now return to our positive point. As we have shown previously, proper means do possess characteristics and are not purely arbitrary labels about which this could not be said. It may help our position to end this chapter with a comparison between proper names and numbers which *can* function in a similar way.

If it so happened that all Dartmoor Prison inmates convicted of larceny had the digit 25 prefixed to their prison numbers, all those convicted of arson 26, all those convicted of murder 27, etc., then this numerical system would begin to function in the same way as general names do. It would be self-contradictory to say that the person or object denoted by the number 278532 was not a murderer because this number was assigned by virtue of the fact that the individual designated was a murderer. The connotation of the number determined its denotation. If the prisoner

The Connotation of Proper Names

answering to the number 278532 had not been convicted of murder then we were wrong in prefixing 27 to his number.

Now let us suppose that the above procedure was generally followed in Dartmoor but that one could not be more than reasonably sure that those prisoners with 27 prefixed to their numbers were murderers. The reason for this elasticity was that the warden was capricious and exercised a certain degree of arbitrariness in assigning his numbers. Therefore it would not always be true that prisoners with the digits 27 prefixed to their numbers were murderers. To unsettle matters still further, let us assume that convicts transferred from other prisons where this general numerical scheme was not operative seldom had their numbers changed. The presence of these *immigrants* would also make it impossible to maintain that all 27 prisoners were murderers; 278532 might well be a petty thief. As a final touch let us assume that a prison mascot (a dog or bird, for example) was referred to affectionately as 258024, because this pet had stolen food or had, to someone's mind, the grasping look of a thief.

We could carry this hypothetical situation further, however. I think that one can already see that the numbers in this second prison system are functioning similarly to proper names. If a logician in analysing this scheme said that the numbers had not fixed general meaning and hence had not connotation, or more specifically, that 258024 did not necessarily imply any attributes and therefore had not connotation we would be justified in rejecting his analysis. We should have to say that because *258024 is not a thief* is not self-contradictory, this does not mean that *258024* is a purely arbitrary label or does not possess connotation. Although we must agree that there is a degree of arbitrariness about the system and that foreign elements disrupt the unity, extending the usage beyond the rigid limits imposed by the first numerical system, still we cannot ignore the fact that these numbers are systematized by reference to a certain descriptive framework, i.e. the crimes committed by the bearer of the number.

In the same way there is a class of characteristics connoted by proper names and when the proper name is used without this descriptive meaning it is being inappropriately applied. And it is precisely because proper names are contextually rooted that they possess connotation.

NOTES

Chapter IX

1. Venn, J., *The Principles of Empirical and Inductive Logic*, London, Macmillan, & Co., 1889, p. 185.
2. James, W., *The Will to Believe*, New York, Longmans Green and Co., 1897, p. 3.
3. Benedict, R., *Patterns of Culture*, London, Routledge & Sons Ltd., 1935, pp. 2, 3. See also Montagu, A., *The Biosocial Nature of Man*, New York, Grove Press, Inc., 1956, pp. 74–6.
4. It is a more difficult task in the case of John Barker, a Nordic-Mediterranean type to decide which racial characteristics he will possess. This is why I used pure Nordic, Mediterranean and Proto-Malay types for my examples at this point. However, we can rest assured that he will have a narrow head, white skin and several other characteristics common to Nordic and Mediterranean races, as well as one or another of certain attributes which are not shared outside of the Nordic-Mediterranean group.
5. Kant meant by 'cogitated through identity' that the predicate-concept is identical with some part of the subject concept.
6. Keynes, J. M., *Formal Logic*, London, Macmillan & Co., Ltd, 1906, p. 18.
7. Bosanquet, B., *Logic*, Oxford Univ. Press, 1911, p. 44.
8. Schiller, F. C. S., *Formal Logic*, London, Macmillan and Co., Ltd, 1931, p. 38.
9. Black, M., 'Vagueness: An Exercise in Logical Analysis', in *Language and Philosophy*, New York, Cornell Univ. Press, 1949, p. 33.
10. Russell, B., 'Vagueness', *Australasian Journal of Philosophy*, Vol. 1, No. 2, June, 1923.
11. Cf. Martin, C. B., *Religious Beliefs*, Cornell Univ. Press, 1959, p. 54.
12. Bradley, F. H., *Principles of Logic*, Oxford, 1922, p. 170.

Chapter X

THE CONCEPT OF GOD

I believe that I have demonstrated by the preceding argument that proper names do possess connotation. Therefore, the principal argument denying that goodness is essential to God on the basis of the impossibility of proper names (like *God*) possessing connotation is untenable. If *God* is employed as a descriptive term (as I believe it usually is), then the entire problem of course does not arise; the logical objections previously described will not be relevant.

Now that this logical objection is overcome, let me reiterate the original argument which, it seems, has considerable merit. Bear in mind that I am *describing* this argument and displaying its logical relevance to the naturalistic fallacy; however, I am not necessarily committed to it. I believe that the theologian who adopts this position can successfully combat Hume's objections; however a considerable theological structure would have to be assumed in advance. It is not within the scope of this book to examine this surrounding framework.

The argument previously mentioned runs as follows: Any act commanded by God is *ipso facto* good. An act is neither made good by God's willing it, nor willed by God on the basis of its objective value. Rather the concept of goodness is an integral and intrinsic constituent of the concept of God, so that if we believe that God wills certain actions it follows that these actions are necessarily good.

To the philosopher who contends that we must be supplied with the proposition: *Whatever God wills is good* before concluding *X is right* from *God wills X*, the theologian can reply that a moral assessment of God's character or conduct is inappropriate and superfluous. The notion of God contains the notion of goodness.

It is not that we are confronted with an enthymeme, the concealed premise of which need not be brought to the surface, but that the argument is already complete without this judgment. Neither is it the case that the major premise of the syllogism is spiritually apprehended rather than the object of a moral judgment (for this would merely alter the epistemological character or form of the major premise without challenging the necessity of the logical sequence), but that it is superfluous to the certainty of the conclusion.

Let me put the same point in more modern linguistic form: The proposition *Whatever God wills is good* is not required because goodness is essential to God by definition. *God is good* is on this reading an analytic proposition; its truth or falsity is discoverable through an analysis of the subject. The predicate is actually unnecessary to a real or theoretical intelligence possessing a comprehensive understanding of the subject; the idea distinctly expressed in the predicate was implicit in the subject. It would be grossly self-contradictory to declare that God is not good.

Before concluding I would like to examine two additional objections to the above conclusion and attempt to refute them.

A: COMPARATIVE CONCEPTIONS OF DEITY

A student of anthropology or sociology might well challenge the notion that *God is not good* is a self-contradictory assertion. He would point out that other gods, particularly those of uncivilized peoples, have occasionally been envisioned and haltingly conceived as malevolent, irascible beings, whom mankind must assuage and propitiate through sacrifice, prayers, offerings and complex ritual, or try to manipulate through magical charms, spells and incantations. To such cultures as the Maori, the Fijians, the Santal of India, the Kogsoagmiut Eskimos, the Coroados of Brazil, and the Gold Coast tribes, it would be true that *the Gods* were quite categorically evil in nature. They upset canoes, destroy the crops through pestilence and storm, frighten game away before the hunter, cause women to be barren, and bring disease and death to the tribe for no apparent reason.

Even the gods of a higher civilization such as that of ancient Greece were not good or just deities in the full moral sense of these terms, although they might be regarded as beneficent beings. For they conferred blessings on those who by worship, power, bribes, or a display of Homeric virtues, secured their good will, but took swift revenge on those who neglected them or even committed offences against them accidentally. (It was, in fact, as a reaction against this doctrine that later Christian theology declared evil to lie in the intention or contemplation of an action, rather than the unwitting perpetration of it.) In many cases, as a result of petty jealousies, promiscuous intrigues, or sheer egotistical envy, they actually displayed malevolent conduct by seducing men into sin or inflicting unjust harm upon them. The Olympian life of the gods certainly could not excite moral admiration even in the Greek mind when Zeus himself 'breathed against his enemies a destructive wrath' when they committed trivial sins against his person.

It must be said, of course, that the conventional opinion about the Olympian deities was not shared by the intellectual leaders. For example, Plato never regarded Zeus as deficient in moral fibre. His apparent malevolence was actually the administration of just punishment to the wicked. Euripides affirmed that 'none of the gods is bad', and that 'if the gods do aught that is base, they are not gods'. And Plutarch strongly asserts that God is certainly not wanting in justice and love, 'the most beautiful of virtues and the best befitting the Godhead'. In general, however, the Greek deities like the Greek heroes were powerful figures not necessarily just ones.

Now to reduce the force of this objection let me point out that although the history of religion does occasionally reveal primitive belief in an evil God, this is perfectly natural. It is to be expected because savage man constructed his gods largely out of the fabric of his own character and his experience of the overwhelming powers of nature. That is, just as he was led to believe in the existence of a beneficent God by attributing his own good conduct and the favourable occurrences of nature to the will of a supreme deity, so he fancied a malicious demon as the source of his evil passions and the destructive natural happenings.[1] (We still commit what has been termed the *pathetic fallacy* on occasions when we speak of the *cruel mountain*, the *friendly river* or the *good earth*. This language is harmless as modern poetic metaphor but in the primitive mind it was the outgrowth of animism, totemism, or the belief in gods with corresponding characteristics.) It is actually quite surprising that nature-religion (and the totemism which, according to Jevons, preceded it) did not lead to a more widespread belief in the malevolence or deity or to a dualistic system of good and evil gods. For the maleficent forces of nature seem to balance or outweigh the beneficent. However, this kind of dualism appears comparatively rarely, the Mazdeism of Persia being the conspicuous example. (It must be remembered in this connection that any deity to which prayers for aid are directed must possess some degree of mercy, compassion or benevolence in his nature for otherwise the prayers would be pointless.)

All of this, of course, is by the way. The real refutation of this anthropological point can take either one of two forms.

First we might indicate that in primitive and natural religion it is only the minor deities which are sometimes regarded as malevolent. Farnell points out '... it is a fact of great significance that the history of religions nowhere presents us with the phenomenon of a High God conceived as malevolent and definitely accepted by the worshipper as such ...'[2] This conclusion is reiterated by Schmidt and Rose: 'As regards morality, the primitive Supreme Being is without exception unalterably righteous; his only connexion with anything morally bad is to abhor and punish it. The true source of this deeply moral character of the Supreme Being is the fact that he is the first and highest, the giver of the moral law, and consequently its origin: ... For the very reason that all evil is kept far from the Supreme Being, those peoples which lay especially great emphasis on his moral character oppose to him another being who is representative of evil, who meets all his endeavours for good with protests and hindrances. We cannot properly call this dualism, for the good Supreme Being is represented as far the stronger and more important; but the origin and continuance of the evil being is often shrouded in a dim twilight which our present knowledge does not allow us to brighten.'[3]

This general notion, however, that a malevolent 'High God' simply does not appear in primitive religion is quite problematic. In the light of this uncertainty a second refutation of the anthropological point seems more forceful.

The modern theologian might well wish to restrict the term *God* to the being conceptualized in the Hebraic-Christian tradition. That is to say, he might well claim that he is not concerned with the general name *God* referring to the deity which has been worshipped anthropomorphically, animistically, or polytheistically in primitive religions, but rather the singular term as it refers to the being who is the object of monotheistic belief.

He would argue that although sophisticated religions like Christianity cannot be severed from rudimentary ritual and belief, some of which did, perhaps, believe in a malevolent High God, or a polytheistic system in which some deities were regarded as evil, even the most hardened sceptic will allow that a higher development of religious thought has occurred in present conceptions of the Godhead. Christians could justifiably assert that the God whom they worship, this conception which has evolved from the gropings of primitive mentality, bears precious little similarity to crude objects of belief such as these. The Christian would further maintain that definite conceptual progress has been achieved; that the stutterings of man in his infancy were more cogently and correctly articulated in the utterances of later thought—utterances which, among other theological notions, attested to the essential goodness of the one God.

From a linguistic viewpoint we could say that for the Hebraic-Christian group of language users *God* is most assuredly applied to an omni-good deity. The notion of goodness is regarded as essential to the concept of deity within this tradition, although goodness may not be contained in the definition of other gods.

B: ANALYTIC PROPOSITIONS: REAL OR VERBAL

Another disquieting objection to my argument states that all that has been demonstrated is that *God is good* is logically and verbally an analytic proposition. No ontological implications can be said to follow from this and my account stands criticized in the same way that I criticized other accounts of the logical behaviour of religious language. (Cf. Chapter VII, B.) In order to attempt to refute this objection I shall have to indicate rather briefly the more comprehensive question involved, namely, the question concerning the nature of analytic propositions.

There is, in fact, a well-known philosophical dispute concerning analytic propositions. On the one hand it is asserted that analytic propositions are logically and metaphysically necessary statements about the essential features of reality. They concern such things as universals, space, time, numbers, abstract objects, etc. However, a number of recent writers have maintained that analytic propositions gain their necessity by being descriptions of verbal conventions. *All fathers have children*, for example, tells us less about the universe than about the way that the term *father* is employed in English usage. Wisdom has written, 'Logically necessary statements are checked by the actual usage of language and to this extent may be true or false'.[4] Ayer's relevant statement concerning analytic propositions is that 'they simply record our determinations to use words in a certain fashion',[5] and at another point that 'they call attention to linguistic usages'.[6] Other writers have added similar testimonies which in effect declare that analytic propositions are thinly disguised synthetic ones; they merely state a fact about general linguistic usage—they are translatable into contingent, empirical propositions concerning the usage rules for terms.

Now it seems obvious to me that there is a class of analytic propositions of which the above remarks are not legitimately applicable. Surely a number of analytic propositions are not of a purely verbal kind, e.g. *I cannot be in Chelsea and Kensington at the same time*, *The square of the hypotenuse of a right-angled triangle is equal to the sum of the square of the other two sides*, *A surface*

The Concept of God

cannot be both red and white all over, Every effect has a cause. In other words there do seem to be a number of logically analytic propositions which cannot be construed as necessarily true according to certain linguistic rules. Rather they are true analytic propositions in a metaphysical sense.

However, having said this, it must be admitted that there also exists a body of analytic statements whose truth is relative to a given linguistic context. For example, *Stealing is blameworthy* is a true analytic proposition in Western civilizations but not a necessary proposition at all among the Dobu Islanders. *All intelligent people have high verbal ability* is a true analytic proposition in the United States and England today; however, if concern over I.Q. testing techniques continues to grow among professional psychologists, this proposition could be falsified shortly and another analytic proposition substituted.

It seems to me that *God is good* as treated in this thesis and as it appears in the Christian theological framework cannot be treated on a purely verbal and logical level. Not all theologians would want to regard this proposition as an analytic one; however, if it is treated in this way it must be regarded as a *real* analytic proposition rather than a verbal one. A necessary *and* metaphysical truth is being asserted about the universe.

NOTES

Chapter X

1. The Enlightenment thinkers, eager for emancipation of the human spirit from convention and prejudice, claimed that religion was nothing more than this sort of anthropomorphic fantasy. They argued quite persuasively that God did not possess ontological status as was traditionally believed, but was a constructed image of our characters—a projection of our self-images raised to superlative conditions of character. Our goodness became infinite goodness when ascribed to God; our love, unending love; our power, omnipotence, etc.
2. Farnell, L. R., *The Attributes of God*, Oxford Univ. Press, 1925, p. 165.

3. Schmidt, W., and Rose, H. J., *The Origin and Growth of Religion*, London, Methuen & Co., Ltd., 1931, pp. 271–2.
4. Wisdom, J., 'Metaphysics and Verification', *Mind*, Vol. XLVII, No. 188, October 1938, p. 463.
5. Ayer, A. J., *Language, Truth and Logic*, p. 114.
6. *Ibid.*, p. 105.

Appendix
AN ANALYSIS OF THE KEY TERMS INVOLVED

In the preceding writings, the reader doubtless noticed that the linked terms *fact/value*, *is/ought* and *descriptive/normative* were used interchangeably. This procedure may strike some as illegitimate owing to the subtle yet vital differences felt to exist between the groups and members involved. They will argue that *description* is not equivalent to *fact*, any more than *norm* is synonymous with *value*; that *is/ought* is not equal to *descriptive/normative*; that *fact* is not to *is* as *value* is to *ought*, and so on.

Since I substituted each set of terms for the other throughout these pages, on the assumption that they did admit of mutual substitution, it seems necessary as a postscript to justify this claim.

Let us therefore first examine the relationship between *fact*, *is* and *description* for the purpose of determining whether or not they can be identically equated, and if not, whether the similarity which they bear to each other is of such a nature that, for our present purposes, we were justified in using them interchangeably.

A: 'IS', 'FACT' AND 'DESCRIPTION'

At first glance, perhaps due to the imprecise manner in which these terms are employed in popular communication, a strong resemblance will immediately be felt between them. To use *fact* for what *is* and what *is* for *description*, does not jangle as discordantly upon our mind's verbal attunement as, for example, using *lemon* for *orange* and/or *orange* for *lime*.

For although we vaguely grasp the generic root, the common denominator appropriate to these latter terms, we would feel exceedingly disinclined to employ them interchangeably—except in specialized circumstances (e.g. we could properly offer the orange, the lime or the lemon when asked for an example of a citrus fruit). The reason for our unwillingness springs from our clearer perception of the nature of the differences and similarities which exist between these fruits. All benefits of empirical differentiation aside, we know that each fruit resembles the others in that it belongs to the same class of edible vegetable product. They are all, in fact, examples of the type of natural object which has been formally classified by botanists into the genus of citrus fruits. Thus it is that although occasions may arise when an orange or a lemon may be physically or verbally offered for each other as instances of their common class, there is an adequate awareness of their relationship to place them in proper perspective, thereby avoiding any of the cognitive errors often engendered by such linguistic confusions. To put this in more technical jargon, the class of citrus fruits is seen to exceed and include the class of oranges and lemons just as the class of oranges is easily viewed as not being co-extensive with the class of lemons.

To take a second example, at the other end of the scale, linguists and trilingual persons would feel little if any hesitation at pronouncing *book*, *libro* and *livre* to be synonyms. For, assuming that inter-language synonyms are possible even though intra-language synonyms are not,[1] these words have the same extensional meaning; i.e., a word-for-word correspondence exists between the three languages at this point, in so far as cultural variations in the denotative application of nomenclature will permit. If a simple 'ostensive definition' experiment were conducted among men already conversant with the idea of symbolization, such that a Frenchman and a Spaniard were brought into the presence of the object which we have labelled *book*, and asked to name it, they would immediately reply *livre* and *libro* respectively.

The question then confronting us is whether *is*, *fact* and *description* fall more into the category of the former example, that is, possess a generic similarity, the non-perception of which has allowed to flourish our mistaken propensity to regard them as identical in meaning with each other; or whether they are in fact identical in extension in the sense in which *book*, *livre* and *ibro* are synonymous. (Not that these two possibilities are mutually exclusive answers to our problem; they merely comprise a *contextual disjunct* which I have posed as a possibly fruitful toehold for our speculation.) In pursuit of this identification and categorization let us first look at the various meanings of the word *is*, in an attempt to indicate the sense intended when it is used in place of *description* or *fact*.[2]

The word *is* is fairly fraught with ambiguity and has provided a fertile ground of exploration for logicians and semanticists alike (particularly general semanticists of the Korzybski school).[4] It is usually accorded three main and distinct meanings: the *is* of identity (*God is the ruler of the universe*), meaning *is identical with*; the *is* of predication (*God is good*), meaning, God has the characteristic of goodness; and the *is* of existence (*God is*), meaning, He has ontological status.[5]

Bertrand Russell, however, is fond of speaking of a timeless *is*, 'like the *is* in *4 is twice 2*', as opposed to its syntactical use, denoting the present tense (although both of these could be subsumed under one or the other of the above meanings, being merely the grammatical—or non-grammatical—aspects of them). Bennett and Baylis have described four additional senses of *is*.[7] First

An Analysis of the Key Terms Involved

they divide the *is* of identity into that of equality and equivalence, symbolized by an equal sign (=) and a tilde (∼) respectively. They also point out the meaning of *is* as 'implies ... as in the pessimistic statement *Living is suffering*' (although I strongly suspect this is really a class-inclusion statement of the sort, *any case of living is a case of suffering*). The use of *is* in the plural as indicating 'a relation of inclusion between classes of objects, as in such expressions as *All prime numbers are natural numbers*'; and the assertional significance of *is* as conveying that 'the writer or speaker believes or asserts what he has just stated'.[8]

Fact likewise has several, if more closely allied meanings, which have been presented in various ways: e.g. 'Actual individual occurrence. An indubitable truth of actuality. A brute event. Syn. with actual event.'[9] '(1) State of affairs (Sachverhalt): an object having categorical—syntactical structure. (2) (*a*) that which simply is, as contrasted with that which is necessary;[10] (*b*) that which is actual as contrasted with that which is merely possible; (*c*) that which is, regardless of its value.'[11] 'Perpetration of act, occurrence of event; thing certainly known to have occurred or be true, datum of experience, e.g. *the fact that fire burns*'[12] 'An objective datum of experience (1) Such expressions as the *universe* or *world* or *thing of fact* all emphasize ... contrast with spheres of desire, value, discourse, etc., which implicate attitudes or constructions on the part of the observer.'[13]

Other writers have reached very different conclusions about *fact* than the above. Whitehead, for example, deposes *fact* from its empirical anchorage and places it in a dependent position when he says, 'In the Universe the status of the World of Fact is that of an abstraction requiring for its concrete reality, Value and Purpose. . . .'.[14] Russell also chips away at the usual image of *fact* by attacking its conception as being empirically verified, in his notion of 'unobserved facts' by virtue of which sentences are true; that 'Facts are wider (at least possibly) than experience'.[15] Both of these are, of course, unusual approaches, the logical consequences and peripheral ramifications of specific philosophical systems.

Perhaps the most widely discussed or disputed senses of *fact* concern whether *fact* should be applied to objects in the universe, such as bicycles, Mr Churchill and kangaroos, or whether this term should be reserved for the properties of these objects, their relationships or their existential status. G. E. Moore, for example, tacitly supports the latter view when he uses the name fact to stand for the 'constituents of the universe which correspond to true beliefs.' He adds, however, probably to forestall criticism, 'I don't mean to say that this is the only sense in which the word *facts* is commonly used. Philosophers, at all events, certainly sometimes use it in a wider sense: they will say for instance not merely that the existence of lions is a fact, but that a lion itself is a fact.'[16] Bertrand Russell also supports this interpretation of fact. 'When I speak of a *fact*, I do not mean one of the simple things in the world; I mean that a certain thing has a certain quality, or that certain things have a certain relation. Thus, for example, I should not call Napoleon a fact, but I should call it a fact that he was ambitious or that he married Josephine.'[17] (These two philosophers later part company over the relation of facts to propositions, Moore claiming that a true proposition is *a fact* or *a reality* and Russell thoroughly separating facts from propositions.)

Returning now to our main point, obviously the *is* of identity as in *God is the ruler of the Universe*, cannot be equated with *fact* as a *brute event*, any more than the *is* of predication as in *God is good* can be said to even roughly correspond to *fact* as it is epistemologically interpreted, e.g. '. . . thing certainly known to have occurred or be true . . .,' or 'an actuality as contrasted with a possibility, a necessity . . .,' etc. However, the *is* of existence can, I believe, be substituted with impunity for *fact* interpreted as, 'An objective datum of experience,' or 'an actual event'; or fact interpreted either as a simple existent thing itself, like *The fact of fire*, or as a characteristic relation, etc., of an existent object, like '*The fact that fire burns*'.

This is in no way an odd or unusual interpretation of the term, picked out of some remote corner to suit our needs. It is the traditional interpretation of fact; the one that was presupposed by Nineteenth Century Subjective or Epistemological Idealism (Eighteenth Century Acosmism), and Realism, in their dispute over whether the world of *fact* has any existence or reality apart from the relation of being perceived or thought (whether facts are *noetic* objects). It is the interpretation of *fact* which is generally differentiated from interpretation in that basic and highly important distinction in the theory of knowledge between what a man senses and what he perceives.

In short, the *is* denoting an existent thing or realm and the *fact* denoting an existent thing or realm can for all practical purposes be treated as equal (grammatical noun and verb differences notwithstanding), and it is this meaning of the respective terms which is intended or assumed when substitution occurred in the previous pages.

The examination of the term *descriptive* or, to use a more easily handled form, *description*, is much less difficult since it really has only one philosophical meaning. This single meaning is adequately put by Professor R. Adamson as follows: 'The statement of the distinctive marks of an object, the marks being of such kind as can be presented in direct perceptive experience.'[18]

The objection which immediately springs to mind against equating description, so defined, to *is* and *fact* is that a statement of the distinctive marks of an object is not the same thing as a word or phrase designating an existential object or state of affairs. That is to say, description is a more *collective* term which stands for a more or less orderly listing of facts (or things that simply *are*), which usually serves to characterize the object in question. Existential facts comprise a description and description*s* are more than one set of facts. That ice is relatively hard is a fact; but that it is hard, has the chemical com-

An Analysis of the Key Terms Involved

position of H_2O, is greyish-white in colour, and melts at above 32°F., is a partial description. (A description of the object *ice*, that is, as differentiated from a definition of the word.)

Yet when philosophers speak of *the descriptive* as contrasted with *the normative*, they do not entertain any thoughts of grammatical number which would induce them to reflect upon whether description should be singular or plural. This consideration is at best irrelevant for their purposes and at worse badly misleading. For the philosophical usage of *description* supersedes these grammatical conventions, since it refers to a broad stratum of the universe; the sphere of existent things. This sphere can be referred to just as well by speaking of *the category of the actual, the world of fact, the existential realm, the descriptive element* or a number of other words and phrases. To say something of the nature of *facts not fact is equal to description* is to fail to comprehend the sense in which *description* is being used.

Once this objection is set aside, and the meaning of *description* made clear in the process, I believe it becomes apparent, without my having begged the question, that *description* can be used interchangeably with *is* and *fact* as previously defined.

Having now discussed the several meanings appropriate to each of the terms under examination, designated the meaning which they hold in common and affirmed their interchangeability by virtue of this matching meaning, it now remains to explain the sense in which we are justified in freely substituting any one term for either of the other two.

It would be blatantly incorrect to assert that *is, fact* and *description* are all identical in the same way that the inter-language synonyms *livre, libro* and *book* are *identical*. Our terms obviously do not bear that great a degree of similarity. Neither can we justify equating *is, fact* and *description* by reference to their being particular instances of some more inclusive category, as the aforementioned *lime, orange* and *lemon* are instances of citrus fruits. Our terms bear a different and much closer relationship than that of being members of a common class.

Then in what sense is it legitimate to regard these words as mutually substitutional? Simply by virtue of their having a meaning in common which is so very similar, bears so close a correspondence, that saying the one is tantamount to saying either of the others; that saying the one virtually *amounts to the same thing* as saying either of the others. Or put in another way, the differences between the respective meanings are so slight as to be negligible for our intents and purposes.

Leibniz claims that objects are identical when they possess the same properties.[19] Perhaps the criterion for words should read that words correspond exactly, when they possess the same meaning. If so, *is, fact,* and *description* as herein treated, bear a high degree of correspondence. It is this correspondence which supplies us with our warrant to use the words interchangeably.

B: 'OUGHT', 'VALUE' AND 'NORMATIVE'

The terms *ought*, *value* and *normative* are enjoying extreme popularity in present-day moral philosophy. This situation both helps and hinders our cause. Our task is considerably complicated by not having a time-moulded, traditional or standard group of meanings to which we can refer; yet by the same token, the fresh diversity and number of interpretations present us with bountiful sources from which to draw.

However, the briefer treatment which these terms will be assigned, as compared with that given to the previous set, is not due to either of these factors. It is due to the fact that our previous discussion has already cleared considerable debris from our path, so that we can proceed directly to the heart of the matter with few, if any, digressions for rendering an explanation, justification or reservation. Let us begin then with the term *ought*.

This term is commonly employed by philosophers and theologians as a verb expressing duty or obligation of a moral sort. (As a noun it is that which is denoted by the verb ought, i.e. duty or obligation.) An example (of the verb) would be: *We ought to love our neighbours*.

Ought is also used without any obligatory content to stand for a state of affairs the existence of which would be a good thing; e.g. *Our team ought to win this match* can be translated into: *It would be a good thing if our team won this match*. (I am assuming that this is not a case of predictability or expectation based upon past performance.) This sense of *ought*, however, is not a moral one since the term *good* in *it would be a good thing . . .* only expresses my personal preference for one sort of outcome rather than another. I would be pleased if our team won the match.

There is another sense of *ought*, which expresses that some humanly controllable fact ought or ought not to be or to have been. An example of an *ought not* of this nature would be: *There ought not to be any natural evil in the world*. This use of *ought* can be considered as indicating a lapse in moral duty on the part of God or some cosmic force capable of altering this state of affairs, or it may be nothing more than a non-condemnatory, empty wish that the present conditions did not exist.

Ought is also used to indicate shortcoming as in: *You ought to know better*; in place of advisable as in *You ought to take more exercise*; to denote what is 'befitting, proper or naturally expected'.[20] As in: *One ought to wear high-heeled shoes to a cocktail party*; and in order to express expectation based upon a strong degree of probability, as in: *The train ought to arrive shortly*.

It is important to stop for a moment at this point and note the above non-moral senses of *ought*. It is clear that whether one should wear a certain type of shoe to a formal occasion is a matter for etiquette, not ethics, to decide; and in saying that the train ought to arrive shortly, we do not intend to level any moral blame if it is late. We learn from the first, something about the customs

An Analysis of the Key Terms Involved

or mores of Western culture, and for the second, what time or how soon we can expect the train to arrive.[21] So many discussions about the *naturalistic fallacy* (Hume's version) have been vitiated by the failure to distinguish between the moral and the non-moral senses of ought. Since we have been dealing with the *naturalistic fallacy* throughout, it is well to mark this major division.

I do not believe that we need examine the numerous philosophical treatments of *ought* which have filled the pages of philosophers from Aristotle and Kant to Ross, Broad and Hare. Neither do we need to judge whether *ought* entails imperatives, implies can, or should have a deontological (formalistic), teleological or logical application.[22] Not that these issues are not themselves interesting and important, but for our present purposes becoming embroiled in such examinations would constitute a digression or departure from the main stream of thought. We can adopt, as a base for comparison, the alarmingly simple interpretation of *ought* as expressing moral duty or obligation, without going any further into the matter in any direction. When we say a man ought to aid the poor, we mean that it is his moral duty to do so, or that he is under moral obligation to do so.

The term *normative* seems far more difficult to characterize. Numerous philosophers have used the term, yet comparatively few have bothered to define it explicitly. As a result one encounters it springing full grown out of the middle of a paragraph or roughly defined, more or less in passing, in another. Thus usually one must infer from the use of the word in context, just what meaning it is being given. Witness the following extracts:

'Among most contemporary philosophers it now passes for an obvious truth that ethic's . . . task, being normative, is to deal not with *what is* but with *what ought to be*.'[23]

Karl Popper in speaking of the difference between 'natural laws' and 'normative laws' speaks of 'normative laws, or standards, or norms, i.e. rules that forbid or demand certain modes of conduct, or certain procedures; examples are the laws of the Athenian Constitution, or the rules pertaining to the election of Members of Parliament, or the Ten Commandments'.[24]

'Ideally a normative *theory* consists of a set of general principles analogous to the axioms of a geometric system.'[25]

'By a *normative sentence* I mean such sentences such as: *I ought to go*; *It would be a good thing if Iowa lost this game*; *The right thing to do is to keep your promise*. They can perhaps be described as sentences which state that some fact ought to be (or have been). Usually, but not necessarily, this fact is a fact of human behaviour. I would wish to call: *There ought to be no earthquakes or other natural disasters* a normative sentence. On the other hand, I would like to exclude merely causal sentences. I do not wish to call such a sentence such as: *You*

Deity and Morality

ought to install new points (where this is elliptical for, *To get more regular firing of your engine, you ought to install new points*) a normative sentence.'[26]

'... normatives (i.e. sentences containing *ought* as an auxiliary verb) ...'[27]

'Norm is.... The principle, whether truth or mode of reality, which controls action, thought, and emotion, if these are to realize their appropriate ends; ... The norm of thinking is truth; of emotion, the beautiful; of volition, the good. These principles (and their corresponding philosophic disciplines) are hence termed normative. The three normative sciences are thus logic, aesthetics, and ethics.'[28] (This is of course an unusual, teleological interpretation.)

'... moral principles (or what are called normative laws)... function ... to guide our choice between alternative courses of action which result in our taking a decision.'[29]

John Mackenzie speaks of ethics as a 'Normative Science' by virtue of the fact that it 'is concerned with an end or ideal or standard'.[30] R. B. Brandt calls questions like '*What kinds of things are desirable or worth while?* and *Which kinds of acts are morally wrong?* and *Do men possess any inalienable rights?*', the 'normative problems of ethics'.[31]

Finally, there is a group of philosophers who are concerned with whether or not a normative use of a word has imperative or mandatory force, and they centre their definition of normative around this issue. Nowell-Smith puts it this way:

'It is sometimes said that *you ought* (normative) sentences are disguised imperatives and since one of the most frequent uses of the imperative mood is to issue orders, that they are disguised commands.'[32] Raphael, for example, says, 'A *normative* use of a word connotes ... a stimulus to action; it has an evocative or imperative force ... The imperative force is a *demand of reason*, i.e. a prescription of universal application.... Normative judgments depend upon *commands* that are universally legislative.... A command is often limited to a particular occasion, expressing a short-lived desire and referring to an individual action. Normative words express a general policy to be followed in all situations of a similar kind.'[33]

John Laird flatly states that 'All normative sciences contain and have to do with imperatives',[34] while Everett Hall makes the contradictory assertion, 'I do not believe they are in all cases simply weak or polite imperatives. ... There is properly no imperative in the past tense, but there are normatives in this tense.'[35]

In mulling over the main gist of these quotations it seems to me that *ought*

An Analysis of the Key Terms Involved

and *normative* are quite similar in meaning. If we use *ought* in the capacity of a verb, its usual part of speech, it appears that all moral and certain non-moral senses of the verb *ought* provide the medium for the expression of normative principles. *You ought to love your neighbour* and *You ought to use a napkin* are both practical utterances of normative principles; *The team ought to win* and *The train ought to arrive* are not normative expressions, except in a highly strained sense.

If we wanted to begin our comparison between *ought* and *normative* at this point, with a view to establishing the relationship between them, we would reach the following conclusions: That every case of a sentence containing a *moral ought* as the verb, is a case of a normative principle being expressed; and every case involving the expression of a normative principle is one in which ought can occur. (This seems to be by virtue of the regulative or controlling nature of both *normative* and *ought* which renders the former amenable to expression in terms of the latter.)

However, we are principally interested in the relationship between *ought* and *normative* when they are (*a*) used only in their moral senses and (*b*) cut loose from their grammatical bindings and placed on an equal footing. For this is the manner in which they will appear throughout the ensuing discussion and hence the way in which they should be judged now. And judged on these grounds, a different and much closer relationship can be discerned to exist between them.

Normative-sentences and *ought*-sentences, or *normativeness* and *oughtness* (to use an agreeable, old-fashioned form), can then be spoken of interchangeably. We can ask whether a particular value entails *oughtness* or *normativeness*, with either one of the terms being redundant and superfluous in relation to the other. We can speak equally well about whether *ought*-sentences or *normative*-sentences should be given a deontological, teleological or logical application; or debate whether *normative*-sentences and *ought*-sentences have imperative force; or affirm that *normatives* and *oughts* imply *can*. The absence of either term, *ought* or *normative*, neither adds nor subtracts from the full meaning of these issues; and the presence of both terms does not pose any different question or elicit any different sort of reply than that presented or provoked by one. In short, neither a quantitative nor a qualitative disparity is present.

In trying to analyse the reason for the interchangeability of our terms in the above context, it seems to be by virtue of the morally obligatory which they share. And this obligatory or *duty charging* nature is the dominant note or essential characteristic pervading each. Thus we are not asserting their interchangeability according to some trivial, supporting attribute which they happen to share, but in consequence of their common core.

However, there is a larger sense in which these terms coincide in meaning which will become clear once we examine the word *value*.

Value is a term which has recently been placed in a highly important position in ethical discourse. It possesses the advantage of being roughly equivalent to certain moral terms, plus the benefit of having comparative freedom from the psychological and philosophical associations which history has woven around these terms.

Although the careful examination of *value* is of great importance to moral philosophy and theology in general, as it has been said of some of our previously examined terms, for our purposes we need not delve too deeply into its nature. We will use a very general sense of *value* as equivalent to *worth*, *goodness* or *rightness*.

Thus we are using it as an abstract noun designating the property of value or of being valuable, rather than (*a*) as a concrete noun referring to things which possess this property of value, or (*b*) in a form which includes evil or badness, which are spoken of as *disvalue*.

Now it appears far more difficult than any of our tasks before, to try to equate *value* so defined with *normative*; and also impossible to equate it with *ought*. The reader may immediately feel that the question of whether value is obligatory in nature, whether 'Ought belongs to the essence of value' is highly relevant here, and, since it has been decided negatively in most cases, that this serves as a sufficient impasse to deter our efforts.

I do not propose to attempt relating these terms by coming down on the positive side of the fence in this issue (although an excellent case can be, and has been, made to support such a view).[36] Rather, according to the broad interpretation of *value* which I shall be using throughout this treatise, such issues are not legitimate considerations. This issue and similar issues are only relevant to a narrow use of *value*. As Frankena puts it, '*Value* is [here] used more narrowly, being contrasted with rightness. Here the distinction intended is within the *ought* as opposed to the *is* and is between the *good* and the *right*, with *value* taken as equivalent to *goodness*. Then the main problem concerns the relation of value and obligation.'[37] (My italics.)

My broader use of value, the one employed throughout these pages, contrasts value 'with *fact* or *existence*. Here the contrast intended is that of the *ought* versus the *is* and the term *value* is used to cover not only the various kinds of goodness, but also beauty and rightness. And the main problem is that of the relation of value and existence.'[38] (My italics.)

This is the interpretation of value which we have been using and the one which as the above sentences indicate is related to *normative* and *ought*. Thus we can speak of 'the nature and status of value in a world of scientific fact and force'.[39] Or we can speak of *normative* in these terms: 'Reference to a norm may be roughly taken to discriminate the philosophic from the natural sciences. The latter aim simply to describe phenomena and explain them in terms of laws or principles. The explaining principles are, moreover, mechanical, having to do with conditions of manifestation in time. In the philosophic sciences, facts are interpreted with reference to their meaning, or value—

An Analysis of the Key Terms Involved

their significance from the position occupied, or part played by them in the total make-up of experience.'[40] Or, as quoted before, 'The *ought* is distinguished from the *is* as the ideal from the actual. . . .'[41]

Numerous other examples and quotations could be cited; however, I believe these few will convey my meaning sufficiently. With *value* used narrowly, it is almost as distinct from *ought* and *normative* as it is from *fact*. But once granted a broad interpretation, these terms are seen to belong to the same, tight ethical grouping.

It is according to this broad view of all of the six terms which we have examined that W. K. Frankena can speak of the naturalistic fallacy as being connected 'with the notion of a bifurcation between the *ought* and the *is*, between value and fact, between the normative and the descriptive.'[42]

NOTES

Appendix

1. Richard Robinson in his excellent book *Definition*, Oxford, Clarendon Press, 1950, p. 95, has taken the notion that 'there are no synonyms' in the same language to mean that the synonym method of defining a word 'can rarely be practised alone without misleading the learner to a considerable extent'. I would carry the view a bit further and say that a synonym, in the first, precise sense offered by the *Shorter Oxford English Dictionary*, that of '. . . a word having the same sense as another . . .', is an impossibility among most, if not all words if the full meaning of the terms is considered—the full meaning which embraces both their denotation *and* their connotation, in the sense of subjective intension. Two or more words can be identical in reference, in that they denote the same object, area of experience, state of affairs, etc; yet I seriously doubt whether two or more words can possess identical flavourings or associations, the *psychological* meaning or subjective intension of the terms involved. To be loquacious is not the same as to be talkative; a diary is not a journal; a serpent is not a snake; to swoon is not to faint; and even something parallel is not collateral. In fact I fail to see how any words could be said to fall within the category of synonyms, if an exact interpretation and a stringent definition of 'synonym' is applied. It is only when connotation is ignored or taken only in a logical sense as meaning the implication of all or some attributes, or when *synonymous* is more loosely interpreted as, perhaps, *being of the same general sense yet having different shades of meaning*, that the class of synonyms is anything but empty. Obviously as the connotation (in its psychological sense) of words approach zero, as in two-language situations, the appropriateness of applying the label *synonyms* to

them increases. For everything else being equal, the degree of connotation is inversely proportional to the correctness of attributing synonymity to two or more words.
2. Any modern philosopher will immediately ask at this point whether I intend to show how these words should be used or how they are in fact used or how I meant to use them. The answer is that I will designate, among the major senses in which each term is used, the sense which I have been using.
3. Levi, A. W., and Frye, A. M., *Rational Belief*, part i, New York, Harcourt Brace & Co., 1941, p. 82.
4. See Cooley, John C., *A Primer of Formal Logic*, New York, The Macmillan Co., 1949, pp. 120-7 and Lee, Irving J., *Language Habits in Human Affairs*, New York, Harper & Bros., 1941, pp. 225-59.
5. For specialized purposes, a perfectly legitimate distinction can be drawn between an ontological *is* and an existential *is*, but for our present interests this neat distinction need not be observed.
6. Russell, B., *An Inquiry into Meaning and Truth*, London, Allen and Unwin, Ltd, 1940, p. 208.
7. Bennett, A. A., and Baylis, C. A., *Formal Logic*, New York, Prentice-Hall, Inc., 1950 (first ed. 1939), pp. 42-3.
8. Parmenides is perhaps the first unwitting perpetrator of an *is* ambiguity when he said that there could be only one thing in the world, and that this thing could have no special qualities. St. Anselm's *Ontological Argument*, however, contains the most classic failure to differentiate between an *is* of existence and that of predication, as Gaunilo, and later Kant, crushingly demonstrated.
9. Frankena, W. K., *Dictionary of Philosophy*, ed. Runes, D. D., New York, The Philosophical Library, 1942, p. 107.
10. I believe the distinction here is one succinctly formulated by Leibniz when he spoke of *necessary truths* as differentiated from *mere matter of fact*.
11. Cairns, D., *Dictionary of Philosophy*, p. 107.
12. *The Concise Oxford Dictionary*, ed. H. W. and F. G. Fowler, Oxford, Clarendon Press, 1958 (4th ed.), p. 424.
13. Baldwin, J. N., 'Fact' in *Dictionary of Philosophy and Psychology*, ed. J. N. Baldwin, London, Macmillan Co., 1901, Vol. I, p. 368.
14. Whitehead, A. N., *Essays in Science and Philosophy*, London, Rider & Co., 1948, pp. 62 and 70.
15. Russell, B., *An Inquiry into Meaning and Truth*, London, Allen & Unwin, Ltd, 1940, pp. 246 and 305.
16. Passmore, J., *A Hundred Years of Philosophy*, London, Gerard Duckworth & Co., 1957, p. 209.
17. Russell, B., *Our Knowledge of the External World*, London, Allen and Unwin, Ltd, 1926, p. 60.

An Analysis of the Key Terms Involved

18. Adamson, R., 'Description' in *Dictionary of Philosophy and Psychology*, ed. Baldwin, Vol. I, p. 271 (I assume Adamson would admit to his definition microscopic objects which require *extra-neural* instruments to view them).
19. The Principles of Leibniz or the P. L. abbreviation in the annotation of logical proofs.
20. *The Shorter Oxford English Distionary*, ed. W. Little, H. W. Fowler, J. Coulson, Oxford, Clarendon Press, 1955, p. 1392.
21. This is not to say that a *moral ought* sentence does not convey any information. As Hare says in *The Language of Morals*, '... the descriptive or informative function of *ought*-sentences increases in direct proportion to the degree to which the principle is generally accepted or known to be accepted' (p. 159).
22. It might be of interest to mention that the *logical* application of *ought* according to C. D. Broad is '... if a man in fact takes a certain end as ultimate, he ought to adopt such means as will bring it into being, and not do things which will be inconsistent with its realization.'
23. Mandelbaum, M., *The Phenomenology of Moral Experience*, Glencoe, Illinois, The Free Press, 1955, p. 13.
24. Popper, K. R., *The Open Society and Its Enemies*, London, Routledge & Sons, Ltd, 1945, p. 49.
25. Brandt, R. B., *Ethical Theory*, Englewood Cliffs, N. J., Prentice-Hall Inc., 1959, p. 295.
26. Hall, Everett W., *What is Value?* London, Routledge & Kegan Paul, Ltd, 1952, p. 155.
27. *Ibid.*, p. 154.
28. Dewey, J., 'Norm and Normative' in *Dictionary of Philosophy and Psychology*, ed. by J. N. Baldwin, Vol. II, p. 182.
29. Bowes, P., *The Concept of Morality*, London, Allen & Unwin, Ltd, 1959, pp. 85-6.
30. Mackenzie, J., *A Manual of Ethics*, London, W. B. Clive, 1924, p. 4.
31. Brandt, R. B., *Ethical Theory*, p. 295.
32. Nowell-Smith, P. H., *Ethics*, Harmondsworth, Middlesex, Penguin Books, Ltd, 1954, p. 191.
33. Raphael, D. D., *Moral Judgement*, London, Allen & Unwin, Ltd, 1955, pp. 119-21.
34. Laird, J., *A Study in Moral Theory*, London, Allen & Unwin, Ltd, 1926, pp. 51-2. R. M. Hare has been accused of reducing moral judgements to imperative *oughts*; however, Chapter II, Section I of *The Language of Morals* clearly absolves him of this charge.
35. Hall, Everett W., *What is Value? op. cit.*, p. 155.
36. Hartmann, N., *Ethics*, London, Allen & Unwin, Ltd, 1932, pp. 277 ff., and notably R. M. Hare in his thesis of moral judgements being prescriptive judgements. He uses the phrase *universal prescriptivism* extensively

in his second book (unpublished at the time of this writing) to cover the universalizability and prescriptivity of moral judgements. These are of course two different things and cannot be criticized simultaneously as some writers have tried to do.

37. Frankena, W., 'Value' in *Dictionary of Philosophy*, ed. by D. D. Runes, p. 330.
38. *Ibid.*, p. 330.
39. Lepley, R., *The Language of Value*, New York, Columbia University Press, 1957, Preface.
40. Dewey, John, 'Norm and Normative' in *The Dictionary of Philosophy and Psychology*, ed. by J. N. Baldwin, Vol. II, p. 182.
41. Seth, J. and Baldwin, J. N., 'Oughtness and Ought' in *The Dictionary of Philosophy and Psychology*, ed. by J. N. Baldwin, London, Macmillan Co., 1901, Vol. II, p. 251.
42. Frankena, W. K., 'The Naturalistic Fallacy', *Readings in Ethical Theory*, ed. Sellars, W. and Hospers, J., New York, Appleton-Century-Crofts, Inc., 1952, p. 103.

INDEX

Abraham, 48 ff.
Agamemnon, 50
ambiguity, 146–7
analogy, 110
analytic propositions, 69–70, 121 ff., 139 ff., 152, 156–7
Anaxagoras, 25
Angeles, J. de, 78
Anscombe, G. E. M., 46
Anselm, Saint, 33, 34, 67
Aristotle, 18, 67, 101, 119
Atlas, 113–15
Aurelius, M., 17
Ayer, A. J., 119, 156

Bain, A., 129, 130
Banier, A., 101
Barth, K., 21–2, 59, 75, 85
Bateson, G., 138
Benedict, R., 137–8
Bentham, J., 15, 17
Berdyaev, N., 100, 101
Bergson, H., 78
Berkeley, G., 34
Bible, 55, 86, 87, 91, 94, 103, 104, 122
Black, M., 145–6
Blackburn, J., 138
Bonaventure, Saint, 33
Boole, G., 126
Boyer, L., 79, 80
Bradley, F. H., 147
Braithwaite, R. B., 113
Broad, C. D., 21
Browning, R., 95
Brunner, E., 21
Butler, Dom. C., 73
Byron, G. G., 98

Caldwell, E., 28
Calvinism, 22, 29
Carnap, R., 119
Cassirer, E., 106
category-mistake, 68, 69, 112

Catholicism, 54
causation, 25
Christianity, 29 ff., 123, 155, 157
Cicero, 25
coherence theory of truth, 104
Collingwood, R. G., 147
Confucius, 75, 140
connotation, 126 ff., 134 ff., 151
Cooper, J. F., 28
Copernicus, 64
Copleston, F., 115
Cordelier, J., 78
cosmologial proof, 53
Creuzer, F. J., 103
Crombie, I. M., 70, 75, 110
Cyrenaics, 16

Dante Alighieri, 91, 96
Darwin, C., 18 ff., 65
deism, 32, 38
Democritus, 25
Dennes, W. R., 46
denotation, 126 ff.
Descartes, R., 15, 33, 34
descriptive terms, 134 ff., 146
Dionysius the Areopagite, 67
divine commands, 42 ff., 80, 84–6, 99–100, 106, 111, 121 ff., 151 ff.
Duns Scotus, 67
Durkheim, E., 20

Eaton, R. M., 127
Emmet, D. M., 111
Empedocles, 25
empiricism, 25, 26, 65, 73
Enemerus, 101
Epictetus, 17
Epicureans, 16
Erigena, J. S., 67
Euripides, 153
evolutionary ethics, 18 ff.
existentialism, 103

173

faith, 48 ff., 58, 59
Falk, W. D., 46
Farnell, L. R., 154
Farrer, A., 96-8, 103
fascism, 106
Faust, 46, 48
Festugiere, P., 79
Fleming, W. K., 79
Fowler, J., 129
Francis of Assisi, Saint, 127

Gaunilo, 35
Gellner, E., 28, 118
general meaning, 139 ff.
general names, 130-1, 140
Gilson, E., 111
Gregory, E., 76
Greig, J. Y. T., 30

Haeckel, E. H., 91
Haldane, J. B. S., 20
Hare, R. M., 46
Harnack, C. G. A. von, 79
hedonism, 15 ff.
Hegel, G. W. F., 33, 49, 90, 102
Heim, K., 68
Hepburn, R. W., 106, 110
Heraclitus, 106
Higher Criticism, 55
Hight, G. A., 95
Hocking, W. E., 78
Höffding, H., 78
holiness, 45, 82
Homer, 95, 96, 101, 153
homonym, 147
Hoskyn, E., 87
Hume, D., 11 ff., 25 ff., 42 ff., 46, 124, 151
Husserl, E. G. A., 116
Huxley, J., 20

image, 90, 91, 100 ff., 114
image-theology, 103-4
ineffability, 73 ff., 111, 114
Inge, W. R., 81
intuition, 80, 93 ff., 114, 123
Iphigenia, 50

irrationality, 51-2, 85, 114, 115
Isaac, 49, 52

James, W., 74, 137
Jevons, F. B., 154
Job, 48
Joseph, H. W. B., 148
Joyce, J., 98-9
Jung, C. G., 105

Kant, I., 34, 35, 37, 46, 102, 123, 141
Keats, J., 98
Kemp-Smith, N., 32, 33, 35
Keynes, J. M., 126, 129, 130, 143
Kierkegaard, S., 48 ff., 80, 110, 114
Klineberg, O., 138
Klubertanz, G. P., 110
Knowles, D., 73
Kropotkin, P., 20

Laird, J., 26, 30
Laredo, B. de., 78
Leibnitz, G. W. von, 33, 47
Leuba, J. H., 78
Lewis, H. D., 94, 105
linguistic analysis, 65 ff., 116 ff., 134 ff.
logical parallels, 110 ff.
logical positivism, 65, 102, 112
logically anomalistic language, 110 ff.
Lotze, R. H., 78
Loyola, Saint, 82
Lytthens, H., 110

Mace, A. C., 129
Machiavelli, N., 82
MacIntyre, A. C., 12, 76, 87, 110, 113
McPherson, T. H., 86
Maritain, J., 111
Marx, K., 127
Mascall, E. L., 110, 115
Mazdeism, 154
Mead, M., 138
Mediaeval theology, 58 ff., 67, 124
Meinong, A., 116
Mill, J. S., 17, 126, 128-9, 131, 148
Milton, J., 91, 96, 97
miracles, 30-1
Moore, G. E., 13-14

Index

Morgan, A. de, 126
Müller, P. E., 101
Murdoch, I., 13
Murray, A. V., 46
Murray, J. M., 94
mystery, 75, 79–80, 82, 84
mysticism, 73 ff., 124
myth, 81, 100 ff., 113, 114

natural theology, 37, 117
naturalism, 25, 26–8
naturalistic ethics, 15 ff.
naturalistic fallacy, 11 ff., 29, 44, 92, 151
nature theories, 17 ff.
Nettleship, R. L., 76
Nielson, K., 43–4, 46, 125
Nietzsche, F., 19, 20, 106, 127
Norris, F., 28
numinous, 84 ff.

Oakeshott, M. J., 147
Oedipus, 47
ontological argument, 33–5, 121
ontology, 111 ff., 156
Osuna, F. de, 76, 78
Otto, R., 84 ff., 99, 114

Paley, W., 21
paradox, 48, 49, 51
Parmenides, 106
pathetic fallacy, 154
Paul, Saint, 48, 59
phenomenalism, 25, 26
piety, 45–6
Plato, 17, 18, 46, 64, 68, 92, 95, 116, 153
Plé, A., 79
Plutarch, 153
poetic language, 77, 78, 90 ff., 111
poetry, 90 ff., 106, 114
Pontifex, C. M., 110
Pratt, J. B., 78, 81–2
prayer, 60, 152 ff.
primitive religion, 152 ff.
Prometheus, 46, 47, 101
proper names, 126 ff., 134 ff., 151
prophets, 96, 98, 124

Protestantism, 54, 85
Proust, M., 82
Pyrrho of Elis, 28
Pyrrhonism, 28, 29

Quietism, 77–8

Ramsey, I., 68, 114, 117
rationalism, 51–2, 58, 62, 78–81, 93
Reardon, B. M. G., 81, 102
Récéjac, J. E., 76
religiouse discourse, 42 ff., 65 ff., 73 ff., 90 ff., 110 ff., 156
revelation, 48 ff., 58 ff., 80, 93 ff., 104, 105, 122
Rose, H. J., 154
Rousseau, J. J., 28
Russell, B., 80, 112, 116, 126, 146
Ruysbroeck, J. van, 78
Ryle, G., 34–5, 68, 112, 116, 117

Santayana, G., 95
Sartre, J. P., 78
scepticism, 30, 32, 33
Schelling, F. W. J., 101
Schiller, F. C. S., 144
Schleiermacher, F., 85, 86
Schmidt, W., 154
Schoolmen, 60, 67
Scripture, 58, 59, 61, 64, 67, 91, 94, 97, 104, 122
Seneca, 17
Shakespeare, W., 96
Shaw, G. B., 127
Shelley, P. B., 98
sin, 60
singular name, 131
Smart, R. N., 46
Smith, J. M., 115
social approval theory, 20 ff.
Society of Friends, 78
Socrates, 44–5
Spencer, H., 18 ff., 77, 123
Stapledon, O., 20
Stirling, A. H., 31
Stoics, 17, 18, 28
Stutfield, H. E. M., 76

175

symbolism, 75–7, 83, 90, 91, 94, 105, 106, 114
synthetic propositions, 126, 142

Taylor, A. E., 30
teleological argument 35 ff., 53
Tennyson, A., 74–5, 76
Teresa, Saint, 82
Tertullian, 59
Theism, 25, 28 ff., 37–8
theological naturalism, 21 ff., 42 ff., 107
theology, 32 ff.
Thomas Aquinas, Saint, 35, 67, 119
Thomas, J. H., 110
Thoreau, H. D., 28
Thornton, L. S., 103
Tillich, P., 105

Underhill, E., 76, 78, 94
unknowable, 73 ff.

Utilitarians, 17

vagueness, 144–5
Venn, J., 134, 138
verification principle, 65
Voltaire, F., 91

Wellington, A. W., 127
Wells, H. G., 146
Whateley, R., 129
White, A. R., 14
Whitehead, A. N., 26
Wilamowitz-Mollendorf, V von, 95
William of Ockham, 67
Wisdom, J., 156
Wittgenstein, L., 77, 86–7, 114, 116, 118, 126

Zen Buddhism, 77
Zeno, 17
Zola, E., 28